IN VENICE
and in the Veneto
WITH
HENRY JAMES

EDITED BY
Rosella Mamoli Zorzi

DIPARTIMENTO DI AMERICANISTICA,
IBERISTICA E SLAVISTICA

UNIVERSITÀ CA' FOSCARI DI VENEZIA

2005

veneziasupernova

This Jamesian guidebook was published by
The Dipartimento di Americanistica, Iberistica e Slavistica
of the University of Venice, Ca' Foscari, on the occasion of
the Henry James Society Conference:

"Tracing Henry James"
Isola di San Servolo, VIU, July 12-15, 2005.

ACKNOWLEDGMENTS:
The images of this guidebook all come from the Biblioteca Nazionale Marciana.
Our thanks go to Piero Falchetta, the creator of the digital project GEO-WEB of this library,
who has generously identified and provided the images.
Research on the former location of the paintings in the Accademia in James's time was carried
out by Maurizio Zanoni, whom we thank. I would also like to thank Gregory Dowling
and Anthony Marasco, both of our Department, for their great help.
I am grateful to Patricia Curtis and her husband Carlo for their ever-affectionate support
of all of my Jamesian projects.

Graphic project: Pier Giovanni Possamai, University of Venice, Ca' Foscari.

Supernova è un marchio registrato, proprietà di
Supernova Edizioni srl
Via Orso Partecipazio, 24
30126 Venezia-Lido
tel./fax 0415265027
e-mail: supernova@libero.it
website: www.supernovaedizioni.it

Printed by Cartotecnica Veneziana srl
July 2005

ISBN 88-88548-54-8

Table of contents

PRESENTATION

It would, perhaps, be easier to list the Venetian places that Henry James did *not* describe, or allude to, in his letters, notebooks, essays, stories and novels, prefaces, than to try and identify all of the places – quays, squares, palaces, bridges, churches, museums – and paintings, he *did* refer to, briefly or at length.

During his many visits to Venice, from the first in 1869 to the last in 1907, James seems to have wandered all over the city and its islands; partly on foot, - many times by himself – but also in a gondola, a hired one first, and, after 1887 probably mostly in the Curtises' private gondola (which still exists in the Barbaro courtyard), with or without Mr. and Mrs. Curtis, his hosts in the magnificent Palazzo Barbaro from that year onwards. We know that the Curtis gondoliers, Angelo or Tita or Domenico, would take him to the station along the Grand Canal, - James even had a "crash" once (24 July 1892), but nothing really serious happened, - and we know that he went out in the gondola with his hosts and hostesses, the latter including Isabella Stewart Gardner, who rented the Barbaro Palace with the Curtis gondola (and James felt that even his own presence came with palace and gondola: "she seems to think I am 'thrown in'", *Letters III*, 296, July 30, 1890). The leisurely trips around town or to go to museums and churches in the family gondola were in fact the norm at the time, as a gondola, with a "gondoliere de casada", was something one had, if one had a palace.

James seems to have frequented the expected spots – the Piazza with the cafés, Florian in the morning, Quadri for lunch, the Museums - but also places that no longer exist, such as the "Bagni", specifically the Bagni Chitarin – those establishments where one could bathe in "fresh or salt water", or have mudbaths, an extremely popular practice given that most of the good hotels had some kind of baths annexed to the main building. James went to the "Bagni Chitarin"; there were two establishments by this name, and James almost certainly went to the one near the Salute, run by Lorenzo Chitarin; the baths were located in the "vast rooms of the Abbey" (of S. Gregorio, the first building to the right of the Salute Church, looking from the Grand Canal), and they had as an annex "salt baths, floating on the Grand Canal in whose pools bathers derive particular advantage from the flow of water which is the deepest in that part of the said Grand Canal".

As regards what was new in Venice in James's time, one wonders whether James ever went to the movies, which started in Venice on July 9, 1896 (Montanaro, 181): it is unlikely, as the "cinematograph" was considered a lower class entertainment. Lady Layard showed a film to her guests in her Palazzo Capello on the Grand Canal only as late as December 15, 1911, "which was a novelty in a private house".

During his different visits, James seems to have wandered over all of the six *sestieri* of Venice, in addition to the island of the Giudecca, which he could also see from one of the top windows of the Palazzo Barbaro, over the roofs of Dorsoduro and across both the Canal Grande and the Canale della Giudecca; he went also to the farther islands, Murano, Burano, Torcello to the North, Malamocco (on the Lido) and Chioggia to the

South. Some of the poorest areas of the town may have been unknown to him, such as the area of San Pietro di Castello, quite remote, but above all very poor, but not the Cannaregio of the Madonna dell'Orto and the Ghetto, not Castello with the church of the Bragora, not Dorsoduro with the church of the Salute and the Accademia, not S. Polo with his adored Tintoretto at the Scuola di San Rocco, not S. Croce with the Palazzo Capello at Rio Marin, the source of the dilapidated palace of the Misses Bordereau in *The Aspern Papers* (1888).

The streets and buildings of Venice have changed less radically than those of other towns, although one will no longer find the girls filling their "water-pots" at the public fountains, described by Hyacinth Robinson in his letter to the Princess in the novel *The Princess Casamassima* (1886):

> I have seen none of the beautiful patricians who sat for the great painters - the gorgeous beings whose golden hair was intertwined with pearls; but I am studying Italian in order to talk with the shuffling, clicking maidens who work in the bead-factories - I am determined to make one or two of them look at me. When they have filled their old water-pots at the fountain it is jolly to see them perch them on their heads and patter away over the polished Venetian stones (*The Princess Casamassima*, 352).

The place that has changed most - and it changed also between James's first visit in 1869 and the later ones, as he observed - is the Lido. The island has been built all over and even the lonely beaches that reminded James of Newport are now crowded and "social", filled as they are with rows and rows of "capanne", showers, cafés etc. Only the tombs of the ancient Jewish cemetery of the Lido are the same James saw and described in *Travelling Companions,* but the cemetery no longer borders the dunes of the beach.

Six itineraries in the city and five itineraries in the lagoon and to the mainland, plus a "Festa"

In this small guidebook we have tried to organize *six itineraries* in the city, plus *five itineraries* to the islands and to the mainland, where the visitor will be able to look at places mentioned or described by James in different texts: to cut up and disperse a Jamesian text is a crime which we have committed, consciously, in the belief that any loving reader of James will go back to the entire letter, essay, story or novel, after having seen the actual place and read the brief excerpts that must be seen as simple reminders of the whole text. For less "passionate pilgrims" we hope this guidebook will be the starting point for a thorough reading of James's works, were it only the "Venetian" works. No words will describe James's love-affair with Venice, and perhaps your own, as effectively as James's own words:

> It is by living there from day to day that you feel the fulness of her charm; that you invite her exquisite influence to sink into your spirit. The creature varies like a nervous woman, whom you know only when you know all the aspects of her beauty. She has high spirits or low, she is pale or red, grey or pink, cold or warm, fresh or wan, according to the weather and the hour. She is always interesting and almost always sad; but she has a thousand occasional graces and is always liable to happy accidents. You become extraordinarily fond of these things; you count upon them; they make part of your life. Tenderly fond you become; there is something indefinable in those depths of personal acquaintance that gradually establish themselves. The place seems to personify itself, to become human and sentient and conscious of your affection. You desire to embrace it, to caress it, to possess it; and finally a soft sense of possession grows up and your visit becomes a perpetual love-affair (*Venice, 7*).

Eventually, you will find that the "real" Venice does not count so much, since the one created by James's words is the important one. But this literary Venice will influence in turn your perception of the city, and you will enjoy the "real" Venice more deeply.

We have added a chapter on a *festa,* that of the *Redentore,* which takes place every year on the third Saturday in July. A bridge on barges is still built across the Canale della Giudecca, between the Zattere and the Redentore Church, for the pilgrimage of the faithful – and faithless – to the Giudecca, where the tables loaded with food are still placed on the quay just as James saw and described them, for the people to sit out and eat and enjoy the evening air while waiting for the fireworks: the great climax to the feast, with millions of lights rising and falling on the lagoon. The Giudecca was surely visited several times by James, who would go to the "garden of Eden", the garden bought by Mr. and Mrs. Eden in 1883; once he brought back to Venice Mrs. Wiel, the wife of musicologist Taddeo Wiel and the sister of the Baron Wenlocks, in a "sociable sandolo", rather than in a more elegant gondola. The garden still exists, is well looked after, and belongs now to the Hundertwasser Foundation, named after the Austrian artist who owned it.

Practical information

The **time** used by each visitor in following each itinerary will depend on the visitor himself: if he – or she – is content with looking at the façade of a church, it will be shorter; if the visit to the interior of the church is felt as necessary, the itinerary will take longer. A truism, but unavoidable in determining the time to be used in each itinerary. Itineraries can be interrupted and done in two visits. You will have to walk a lot anyhow, but, should you be too tired, there will always be a boatstop not too far away where you can take a boat and return to your hotel or lodgings.

Starting points

We have chosen as starting points two of the five addresses where James stayed at different times, and/or *boatstops* to help you find your bearings and your way. Just remember that

Vaporetto n. 1 goes all the way from the Lido to San Marco to Rialto to the Station, all along the Grand Canal, and viceversa, the main stretch for your purposes being from San Zaccaria or Calle Vallaresso (both in the St. Mark's area) to the Station, with such stops as Salute, S. M. del Giglio, Accademia, Ca' Rezzonico, S. Tomà, S. Angelo, S. Silvestro, Rialto, Ca' d'Oro, S. Stae, S. Marcuola, Riva de Biasio, Stazione.

Diretto n. 82 goes the same way (in the Summer) and only from Calle Vallaresso to the Station in the winter: it is faster and only stops, along the Grand Canal, at Accademia, San Samuele, S.Tomà, Rialto, S. Marcuola (every other boat), Station.

There are *different lines circling the city* (n.41, 42, 51, 52, 61, 62), lines going to Lido (from Riva degli Schiavoni), to Murano, Burano, Torcello (from Fondamente Nuove, on the north side of the city), to Chioggia (boat to Lido, then bus n.11, then boat again). A booklet published by ACTV (Orario/Timetable) can be bought for 0.60 eurocents at major boatstops; it has information on lines, times, and less expensive boat passes.

Tickets: look in the booklet for the different possibilities for a 24-hour (10,50 euros) or 72 hour pass (22 euros) (or ask at major boatstops ticket offices "Vela"). Single tickets are fairly expensive (3.50 eurocents for a ticket, 5 eurocents for the Canal Grande 90-minute ticket) and are more expensive if bought on board the boats.

This is *not* a guidebook to Venice. In addition to the various guidebooks one can find in bookshops, *the* most detailed guidebook to Venice still is the *Venezia e il suo estuario* by Giulio Lorenzetti ("il Lorenzetti"), available in an English translation, sold in bookshops and in the specialized Filippi Bookstore, in Calle del Paradiso, just off the Campo S. Maria Formosa.

A warning

Like James in his essay *Venice,* we will warn you. Before you start, you should be aware that you might be disappointed during your itineraries, especially itinerary 1, the second part of 2, and 3, as they will take you through *very crowded areas* of the city; less so with the first part of itinerary 2 – once you turn your back to the crowds of the Riva degli Schiavoni you will be all right – or itinerary 5:

> The barbarians are in full possession and you tremble for what they may do. You are reminded from the moment of your arrival that Venice scarcely exists any more as a city at all; that she exists only as a battered peep-show and bazaar. There was a horde of savage Germans encamped in the Piazza, and they filled the Ducal Palace and the Academy with their uproar. The English and Americans came a little later. They came in good time, with a great many French, who were discreet enough to make long repasts at the Caffé Quadri, during which they were out of the way. The months of April and May of the year 1881 were not, as a general thing, a favourable season for visiting the Ducal Palace and the Academy. The *valet-de-place* had marked them for his own and held triumphant possession of them. He celebrates his triumphs in a terrible brassy voice, which resounds all over the place, and has, whatever language he be speaking, the accent of some other idiom. During all the spring months in Venice these gentry abound in the great resorts, and they lead their helpless captives through churches and galleries in dense irresponsible groups. They infest the Piazza; they pursue you along the Riva; they hang about the bridges and the doors of the cafés (*Venice,* 7).

James was prophetic in his view of the destiny of the city. Only a few guides use new technology that allows them not to have to cry out in brassy voices, but the herds of "helpless captives" have simply multiplied. If the *valet-de-place* is no longer called by this name, a high number of them still exercize their trade, hooking tourists into glass-factories or restaurants.

However, in spite of mass tourism, in spite of crowds slowly looking at shops more than at churches, you will find yourself at one point, in each of these itineraries, magically in front of a wonderful church, a prodigious crucifixion painting, a little bridge and a pink wall, which will recompense you for having to make your way through slow milling crowds, for having suffered the cold and damp of a secluded church, for having wet your feet and having shivered in the bitter wind (like Penderton in *The Pupil* or like poor Whistler, in real life, whose Venetian winter was so cold that his hands froze on the plates he was holding for his future series of wonderful Venice etchings!) or in the "wicked wind" of *The Wings of the Dove.*

You will be rewarded for having got tired and thirsty on a hot summer day (James could'nt stand the heat either).

When you are back at home, you will shed all your feelings of fatigue, heat, dampness, and you will re-read the Jamesian texts enjoying them all the more, now that you have the memories of what you – and Henry James – saw. This final enjoyment in reading James, or re-reading James, is what this little book aims at.

I simply see a narrow canal in the heart of the city – a patch of green water and a surface of pink wall. The gondola moves slowly; it gives a great smooth swerve, passes under a bridge, and the gondolier's cry, carried over the quiet water, makes a kind of splash in the stillness. A girl crosses the little bridge, which has an arch like a camel's back, with an old shawl on her head, which makes her characteristic and charming; you see her against the sky as you float beneath. The pink of the old wall seems to fill the whole place; it sinks into the opaque water. Behind the wall is a garden, out of which the long arm of a white June rose – the roses of Venice are splendid – has flung itself by way of spontaneous ornament (*Venice*, 13).

Chronology of James's visits to Venice, with addresses:

1869 - September, "Hotel Barbesi", at Palazzo Zucchelli, formerly Badoer-Tiepolo, across from the Salute, on the Grand Canal (S. M. del Giglio, Corte Barozzi, 2161: the door number is no longer visible, but the hotel was where the Westin Europa and Regina is now). There is a Carlo Naya photo of the façade.
The Barbesis owned several hotels, including an elegant one in Palazzo Grassi.

1872 - September, very brief stay with sister Alice.

1881 - March-June, Riva degli Schiavoni 4161, *quarto piano* (fourth floor), now Pensione Wildner.

1887 - February-March, Casa Alvisi, on the Grand Canal, across from the Church of the Salute, a guest of Mrs. Katharine de Kay Bronson (now to the left of the Hotel Europa, looking from the water). Guests actually stayed in the Giustinian-Recanati wing. Mrs. Bronson (1834-1901), American, had moved to Venice in 1875, and lived there with her daughter Edith, born in 1861, who married Count Cosimo Rucellai from Florence.

1887 - June-July, first stay at Palazzo Barbaro (S. Stefano, 2840), on the Grand Canal: you can see it from the top of the Accademia Bridge, turning your back on the Galleries of the Accademia. It is the second palace to your right. The palace is in fact made of two palaces, the first a Gothic one, the second of a later date. Windows of the *piano nobile* closed by wooden boards now.
James's hosts were Mr. Daniel Sargent Curtis (1825-1908) and Ariana Wormeley Curtis (1833-1922), from Newport and Boston, with the occasional presence of one of their sons, the painter Ralph Curtis (1854-1922). In 1892 James was the guest of Isabella Stewart Gardner (1840-1924).

1890 - June, at the Palazzo Barbaro before going to Oberammergau and on the way back, without the Curtises this time.

1892 - July, at Palazzo Barbaro, as a guest of Isabella Stewart Gardner, who put a bed for him in the "divine old library" above the *piano nobile*. In 1892 James identified a place he might like to buy, but did not buy: the house which is now the Fondazione Masieri, at the beginning of Rio Nuovo, on the right of the Ca' Foscari, looking from the Grand Canal: "I came within an ace of taking a very modest one [a little *permanent* perch or asylum] the day before I left – just out the Grand Canal but looking straight into it – a house that faces the side of the Palazzo Foscari", as he wrote to Ariana Curtis on August 16, 1892 (*LPB*, 128).

1894 - April-May, and June-part of July, after a trip to Rome, at Casa Biondetti, small house on the Canal Grande, at San Vio 715. Looking from the water it is the first to the right of the Guggenheim Collection (Palazzo Venier dai Leoni, Dorsoduro 704). It had been Constance Fenimore Woolson's house and James chose to stay there when he was working on Woolson's papers as her literary executor. Woolson (1840-1894) killed herself throwing herself on the street from the windows of the Palazzo Semitecolo (Dorsoduro 187, Calle del Bastion). Palazzo Semitecolo is on the same side of the Canal, towards the Salute; looking from the water it is on the left side of the Palazzo Salviati, which is decorated by a mosaic. On the grand Canal facade of the Casa Biondetti you can see a plaque in memory of painter Rosalba Carriera (1675-1757).

1899 - April-May at the Palazzo Barbaro.

1907 - June, last visit, at the Palazzo Barbaro.

Glossary of Venetian street indications

Ca': as in Ca' Foscari. Usually indicated as short for "casa" (house).
Calle: street.
Campo: small square.
Campiello: smaller square.
Canale: canal.
Corte: small square.
Fondaco: storeroom and living quarters. For instance: Fondaco dei Turchi, Fondaco dei Tedeschi (of the Turks, the Germans).
Fondamenta, pl. Fondamente: quay along a canal.
Liagò: small jutting-out covered terrace, usually made of wood.
Parrocchia: parish (e.g. Parrocchia di Santa Maria Formosa: area of the city linked to the parish church of Santa Maria Formosa).
Piano nobile: main floor in a palace. Often a palace has two piani nobili, on the first and second floors.
Piazza: Square. Only St. Mark's is a piazza, all other squares are called "campi".
Piazzetta: St. Mark's part of the square overlooking the lagoon, where there are the two columns with the Chimera and St. Theodore on the crocodile.
Piscina: an area of filled-in ground where there used to be water (see rio terrà).
Ponte: bridge.
Ramo: side street.
Rio: canal.
Rio terrà: a filled-in canal.
Riva: as in Riva degli Schiavoni, street along the water (quay), or, water entrance to a house.
Ruga: street.
Salizzata: street that has been paved (cfr. Italian "selciato").
Scuola: the word means "school" in Italian, but in our context it indicates a free Association of citizens, for purposes of mutual help and spiritual and religious services. There were six Scuole Grandi, San Marco, San Rocco, San Teodoro, San Giovanni Evangelista, Scuola della Carità and La Misericordia, and over 360 smaller scuole.
Sestiere: one of the six zones into which Venice is divided (San Marco, Castello, Cannaregio, Dorsoduro, Santa Croce, San Polo). To these must be added the islands (Giudecca, Lido, Murano, etc.)
Sottoportico (or **sottoportego**): covered passageway.
Traghetto: gondola ferry across the Grand Canal. There were many more than there are now. The traghetto di San Tomà is among the most active ones:

They [the gondolieri] chatter at the *traghetti*, where they always have some sharp point under discussion; they bawl across the canals; they bespeak your commands as you approach; they defy each other from afar. If you happen to have a *traghetto* under your window, you are well aware that they are a vocal race (*Venice*, 15-16).

Itineraries

Itinerary 1. Around St. Mark's and to the Fenice Theatre.

This is the most obvious and crowded and touristy walk. The enchantment of St. Mark's is perhaps difficult to perceive during the crowded daytime. Go back in the evening when most of the day-trippers are gone, or very early in the morning, or use your imagination.

Starting Point: **Riva degli Schiavoni 4161** (now Pensione Wildner) or boatstop San Zaccaria (any: the one for boats n. 20 to S. Servolo or n. 82 to Tronchetto, near the bridge of La Pietà, or the one nearer St. Mark's).

> I lodged on the Riva, 4161, *quarto piano.* The view from my window was *una bellezza;* the far-shining lagoon, the pink walls of San Giorgio, the downward curve of the Riva, the distant islands, the movement of the quay, the gondolas in profile. Here I wrote, diligently every day and finished, or virtually finished, my novel (*Notebooks,* 221).

James in fact had difficulty in finishing *Portrait of a Lady* (1881), as he later wrote in the *Preface:*

> I had rooms on the Riva Schiavoni, at the top of a house near the passage leading off to San Zaccaria; the waterside life, the wondrous lagoon spread before me, and the ceaseless human chatter of Venice came in at my windows, to which I seem to myself to have been constantly driven, in the fruitless fidget of composition, as if to see whether, out in the blue channel, the ship of some right suggestion, of some better phrase, of the next happy twist of my subject, the next true touch for my canvas, might n't come into sight.
> (…)
> There are pages of the book which, in the reading over, have seemed to make me see again the bristling curve of the wide Riva, the large colour-spots of the balconied houses and the repeated undulations of the little hunchbacked bridges, marked by the rise and drop again, with the wave, of foreshortened clicking pedestrians. The Venetian footfall and the Venetian cry – all talk there, wherever uttered, having the pitch of a call across the water – come in once more at the window, renewing one's old impression of the delighted senses and the divided, frustrated mind (*Preface,* 1070-71).

Look at the Riva and walk along the quay, past the Monumento to Vittorio Emanuele and turn right, under the Sottoportico San Zaccaria and into the Campo San Zaccaria, for a brief visit to the **Church of San Zaccaria.** Look at the beautiful painting by Giovanni Bellini, *Sacra Conversazione,* or *Madonna on the Throne with the Child Jesus, Saints and an Angel Musician* (1505) on the second altar to the left as you enter:

> So too is the Madonna of San Zaccaria, hung in a cold, dim, dreary place, ever so much too high, but so mild and serene, and so grandly disposed and accompanied, that the proper attitude for even the most critical amateur, as he looks at it, strikes one as the bended knee (*Venice,* 25-26).

Piazzetta dal Molo. Giovanni Pividor, *Souvenirs de Venise* (Venice: 1836), plate 6.

You can now see this painting quite well, although it is on the altar where James saw it (look at the carved stone cornices and the corresponding *painted* carved stone cornices in the painting). Walk back to the Riva and walk past the Hotel Jolanda-Savoia, over one bridge (Ponte del Vin): to your right is the **Hotel Danieli**, where Mr. and Miss Evans (*Travelling Companions*) stayed; move on over the Ponte della Paglia into **the Piazzetta**, where Miss Tina landed in her gondola tour with the "publishing scoundrel", after admitting that her aunt had "everything" ("Oh, she has everything!" sighed Miss Tina) as regarded "papers of value" (*The Aspern Papers*):

> These words caused all my pulses to throb, for I regarded them as precious evidence. I felt them too deeply to speak, and in the interval the gondola approached the Piazzetta. After we had disembarked I asked my companion if she would rather walk round the square or go and sit before the great café; to which she replied that she would do whichever I liked best – I must only remember how little time she had. I assured her there was plenty of time to do both, and we made the circuit of the long arcades. Her spirits revived at the sight of the bright shop-windows, and she lingered and stopped, admiring or disapproving their contents, asking me what I thought of things, theorizing about prices (*The Aspern Papers*, 237).

On the right in the Piazzetta is the **Ducal Palace**, where James went several times, and where he enjoyed the light of the serene Veronese contrasting it to the tragic greatness of Tintoretto in the Scuola di S. Rocco; look at the rich rooms where "P. Veronese revels on the ceilings and Tintoret rages on the walls" (*LPB*, 58), in particular, in the Sala dell'Anticollegio, admire the *Rape of Europa* by Veronese and the *Pallas chasing away Mars and protecting Peace and Abundance,* and the *Bacchus and Ariadne,* two of the four paintings by Tintoretto (1578).
This is *The Rape of Europa* by Veronese:

> He [Veronese] was the happiest of painters and produced the happiest picture in the world. "The Rape of Europa" surely deserves this title; it is impossible to look at it without aching with envy. Nowhere else in art is such a temperament revealed; never did inclination and opportunity combine to express such enjoyment. The mixture of flowers and gems and brocade, of blooming flesh and shining sea and waving groves, of youth, health, movement, desire – all this is the brightest vision that ever descended upon the soul of a painter. Happy the artist who could entertain such a vision; happy the artist who could paint it as the masterpiece I here recall is painted (*Venice*, 23-24).

16

Ducal Palace. Antonio Quadri, *La Piazza di San Marco* (Venice: 1831), plate 3.

This is the *Pallas and Mars* by Tintoretto:

"Pallas chasing away Mars" is, I believe, the name that is given to the picture; and it represents in fact a young woman of noble appearance administering a gentle push to a fine young man in armour, as if to tell him to keep his distance. It is of the gentleness of this push that I speak, the charming way in which she puts out her arm, with a single bracelet on it, and rests her young hand, its rosy fingers parted, on his dark breastplate. She bends her enchanting head with the effort - a head which has all the strange fairness that the Tintoret always sees in women – and the soft, living, flesh-like glow of all these members, over which the brush has scarcely paused in its course, is as pretty an example of genius as all Venice can show (*Venice*, 24).

This is again *The Rape of Europa*, followed by the *Bacchus and Ariadne* by Tintoretto, as described by the narrator of *Travelling Companions:*

We went to the Ducal Palace, and immediately made our way to that transcendent shrine of light and grace which contains the masterpiece of Paul Veronese, and the Bacchus and Ariadne of his solemn comrade. I steeped myself with unprotesting joy in the gorgeous glow of salubrity of the radiant scene, wherein, against her bosky screen of immortal verdure, the rosy-footed, pearl-circled, nymph-flattered victim of a divine delusion rustles her lustrous satin against the ambrosial hide of bovine Jove (*Travelling Companions*, 206).

"This, I think, is the brighter dream of the two," she [Miss Evans] answered, indicating the Bacchus and Ariadne. Miss Evans, on the whole, was perhaps right. In Tintoretto's picture there is no shimmer of drapery, no splendor of flowers and gems; nothing but the broad, bright glory of deep-toned sea and sky, and the shining purity and symmetry of deified human flesh. "What do you think," asked my companion, "of the painter of that tragedy at San Cassiano being also the painter of this dazzling idyl; of the great painter of darkness being also the great painter of light?"
"He was also a colorist! Let us thank the great man, and be colorists too. To understand this

Bacchus and Ariadne we ought to spend a long day on the lagoon, beyond sight of Venice. Will you come to-morrow to Torcello?" (*Travelling Companions*, 207).

Maybe James was thinking of another *Bacchus and Ariadne*, when he had Mr. Brooke underline "this" Bacchus and Ariadne; maybe he was comparing it with the one by Titian in the London National Gallery, a painting he loved, and described to John La Farge as "a thing to go barefoot to see".

Stop also in the Sala del Maggior Consiglio and admire the enormous *Paradiso* (1590) by Tintoretto, which for Twain was "Saturday Night in Heaven". For James it unfolded "its somewhat smoky splendour and the wonder of its multitudinous circles".

Once you are outside the Ducal Palace, you can enter the **Church of St. Mark**, if there isn't a long line. The interior of the church always looked to James dimmer and darker than it does today, with its fairly recent lighting system, which is sometimes even too bright:

> Within the church, the deep brown shadow-masses, the heavy thick-tinted air, the gorgeous composite darkness, reigned in richer, quainter, more fantastic gloom than my feeble pen can reproduce the likeness of. From those rude concavities of dome and semi-dome, where the multitudinous facets of pictorial mosaic shimmer and twinkle in their own dull brightness; from the vast antiquity of innumerable marbles, incrusting the walls in roughly mated slabs, cracked and polished and triple-tinted with eternal service; from the wavy carpet of compacted stone, where a thousand once-bright fragments glimmer through the long attrition of idle feet and devoted knees; from sombre gold and mellow alabaster, from porphyry and malachite, from long dead crystal and the sparkle of undying lamps, - there proceeds a dense rich atmosphere of splendor and sanctity which transports the half-stupefied traveller to the age of a simpler and more awful faith. I wandered for half an hour beneath those reverted cups of scintillating darkness, stumbling on the great stony swells of the pavement as I gazed up at the long mosaic saints who curve gigantically with the curve of dome and ceiling. I had left Europe; I was in the East (*Travelling Companions*, 192).

On your way out have a look at the **northern side of St. Mark's** and notice here that wherever "the hand of the restorer has been laid all semblance of beauty has vanished", "giving way to large crude patches of new material which have the effect of a monstrous malady rather than of a restoration to health".

St. Mark: the Basilica. *Ventiquattro vedute principali della città di Venezia* (Milan, Florence, Venice: n.d.), plate 2.

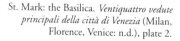

18

It was against this procedure of radical restoration that Ruskin won his battle in Venice. Walk into the Piazza, to your right is **Caffé Quadri**, where James went for a second breakfast (or lunch), and some of his characters for lunch (Mr. and Miss Evans, for instance, upstairs); invest a fortune to eat ice at **Caffé Florian** (on your left as you walk out of the church, Procuratie Nuove 56-59, across from the Quadri), again like Miss Evans (and her would be fiancé) in *Travelling Companions*, like Mrs. Tramore and her daughter in *The Chaperon*, like Hyacinth Robinson in *The Princess Casamassima*, or like the narrator of *The Aspern Papers*:

> After dinner we went down into the Piazza and established ourselves at one of Florian's tables. Night had become perfect; the music was magnificent. At a neighboring table a group of young Venetian gentlemen, splendid in dress, after the manner of their kind, and glorious with the wondrous physical glory of the Italian race.
> "They only need velvet and satin and plumes," I said, "to be subjects for Titian and Paul Veronese." (*Travelling Companions*, 195)

> I sat in front of Florian's café eating ices, listening to music, talking with acquaintances: the traveller will remember how the immense cluster of tables and little chairs stretches like a promontory into the smooth lake of the Piazza. The whole place, of a summer's evening, under the stars and with all the lamps, all the voices and light footsteps on marble – the only sounds of the immense arcade that encloses it – is an open-air saloon dedicated to cooling drinks and to a still finer degustation, that of the splendid impressions received during the day (*The Aspern Papers*, 211).

Walk then through the arches at the end of the Piazza, straight into the Calle de l'Ascensione and take the first street to your right, the Frezzeria. Follow it all along turning left at its end (it continues to be called Frezzeria), cross the Ponte del Barcariol into the narrow Calle del Frutarol. Before entering the Campo San Fantin, turn right into the **Calle Minelli**, where **George Sand** lived with Doctor Pagello, who became briefly her lover, breaking up her relation with de Musset, a story that surely fascinated, and perhaps a little horrified, James:

> Madame Sand's famous Venetian year has been of lately immensely in the air – a tub of soiled linen which the muse of history, rolling her sleeves well up, has not even yet quite ceased energetically and publicly to wash. The house in question must have been the house to which the wonderful lady betook herself, when, in 1834, after the dramatic exit of Alfred de Musset, she enjoyed that remarkable period of rest and refreshment with the so long silent, the but recently rediscovered, reported, extinguished, Doctor Pagello. As an old Sandist – not exactly indeed of the *première heure*, but of the fine high noon and golden afternoon of the great career – I had been, though I confess too inactively, curious as to a few points in the topography of the eminent adventure to which I here allude; but had never got beyond the little public fact, in itself always a bit of a thrill to the Sandist, that the present Hotel Danieli had been the scene of its first remarkable stages (*Two Old Houses and Three Young Women*, 71-72).

La Fenice Theater: backside view. Giovanni Pividor, *Souvenirs de Venise* (Venice: 1836), plate 22.

James was taken to see the house by the "three young women" of the 1899 Venetian essay (identified by Marilla Battilana as the three Mocenigo sisters), but he had already dealt with the subject in 1897:

In the meantime a great deal had happened, for their [Sand and de Musset's] union had been stormy and their security small. Madame Sand had nursed her companion in illness (a matter-of-course office, it must be owned) and her companion had railed at his nurse in health. A young physician, called in, had become a close friend of both parties, but more particularly a close friend of the lady, and it was to his tender care that on quitting the scene Musset solemnly committed her. She took up life with Pietro Pagello – the transition is startling – for the rest of her stay, and on her journey back to France he was no inconsiderable part of her luggage (*George Sand,* in *French Writers,* 744).

Walk back into the Campo San Fantin, where you will see the rebuilt **Fenice Theatre**, where James did go in spite of his declaration: "you have tried the opera and found it very bad" (*Venice,* 5). During his 1881 stay the niece of the pension owner hovered "about the premises in a velvet jacket and a pair of black kid gloves with one little white button", and a lovely oval powdered face, *because* she was a dancer at the Fenice.

La Fenice Theater. *Memorie di alcune più celebri fabbriche e situazioni di Venezia* (Venice: 1831), plate 24.

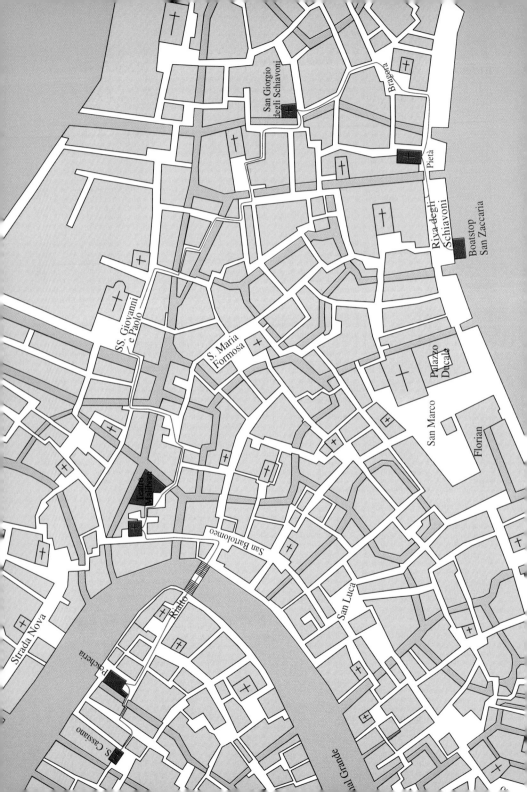

Itinerary 2. Part I. From the Riva degli Schiavoni to SS. Giovanni e Paolo

Starting point: **Riva degli Schiavoni 4161**, now Pensione Wildner or San Zaccaria boatstops (any: the one for boats n. 20 to S. Servolo or 82 to Tronchetto, near the bridge of La Pietà, or the one nearer St. Mark's). Walk away from St. Mark's, along the quay (Riva degli Schiavoni), to the bridge of La Pietà; from the top of the bridge look at the **island of San Giorgio**:

> You soon recognise that it is not only the many-twinkling lagoon you behold from a habitation on the Riva; you see a little of everything Venetian. Straight across, before my windows, rose the great pink mass of San Giorgio Maggiore, which has for an ugly Palladian church a success beyond all reason. It is a success of position, of colour, of the immense detached Campanile, tipped with a tall gold angel. I know not whether it is because San Giorgio is so grandly conspicuous, with a great deal of worn, faded-looking brickwork; but for many persons the whole place has a kind of suffusion of rosiness. Asked what may be the leading colour in the Venetian concert, we should inveterately say Pink, and yet without remembering after all that this elegant hue occurs very often. It is a faint, shimmering, airy, watery pink; the bright sea-light seems to flush with it and the pale whiteish-green lagoon and canal to drink it in. There is indeed a great deal of very evident brickwork, which is never fresh or loud in colour, but always burnt out, as it were, always exquisitely mild (*Venice*, 12).

Don't forget, some day, to take a boat to San Giorgio and look at Tintoretto's *The Last Supper* (see p. 65) and *The Fall of the Manna* (in the church, paintings which James, of course, loved).

After contemplating the lagoon, also imagine the baths which were east of San Giorgio, as represented in the painting *Ritorno dal Lido* (1884) by Ralph Curtis, the types of baths – like the Stabilimento Chitarin – which James used to go to. Walk on past the church of La Pietà (represented in Curtis's painting without its later facade), over the next bridge (Ponte del Sepolcro), look at the plaque in memory of Petrach's Venetian stay, and past the Caserma Cornoldi turn left into the Calle del Dose which will take you straight into the Campo della **Bragora** (or Bandiera e Moro). On your right is the church with two paintings by Cima da Conegliano. The first James mentions is *St. Helen and Constantine on either side of the Cross* (1502), a small painting which is on the right

Church of San Giovanni Battista in Bragora. *Venezia monumentale pittoresca*, II (Venice: 1865), plate 58.

23

wall, near the entrance to the Sacristy (with a *pendant* by Alvise Vivarini, *Christ Resurrected*). The second is *The Baptism of Christ* (1492-94), on the main altar:

> You renounce all hope, for instance, of approaching the magnificent Cima da Conegliano in San Giovanni in Bragora; and bethinking yourself of the immaculate purity that shines in the spirit of this master, you renounce it with chagrin and pain. Behind the high altar in that church hangs a Baptism of Christ by Cima which I believe has been more or less repainted. You make the thing out in spots, you see it has a fulness of perfection. But you turn away from it with a stiff neck and promise yourself consolation in the Academy and at the Madonna dell'Orto (*Venice*, 21).

The fact that James went to see the Cima following Ruskin's preferences appears clearly in *The Chaperon:*

> It had something to do with their going together that afternoon, without her mother, to look at certain out-of-the-way pictures as to which Mr. Ruskin had inspired her with a desire to see sincerely. Mrs. Tramore expressed the wish to stay at home, and the motive of this wish – a finer shade than any that even Ruskin had ever found a phrase for – was not translated into misrepresenting words by either the mother or the daughter. At San Giovanni in Bragora the girl and her companion came upon Mrs. Vaughan-Vesey, who, with one of her sisters, was also endeavouring to do the earnest thing. She did it to Rose, she did it to Captain Jay, as well as to Giambellini (*The Chaperon*, 847).

There is no Giovanni Bellini in the Bragora, but there is a *Madonna with Child* (1485-90), by Alvise Vivarini, across from the *St. Helen,* which might easily be taken for a Bellini. From Bragora (walking out of the church to the right, to the corner of the Campo) take the Salizzada S. Antonin (admire on your left a Gothic palace whose frescoed decoration along the windows James could not have seen: it is a very recent restoration). Walk all the way along the Salizzada to the next bridge (Ponte S. Antonin), don't go over it but turn right along the Fondamenta dei Furlani: at the end of the Fondamenta is the Scuola Dalmata or *S. Giorgio degli Schiavoni;* admire its S. Jerome and St. Agustine on the right, and other paintings by Vittor Carpaccio:

Chiesa di S. Giorgio de' Schiavoni sulla Fondamenta di S. Antonino.

…the noble St. Jerome in his study at S. Giorgio Schiavoni. This latter work is a pearl of sentiment, and I may add without being fantastic a ruby of colour. It unites the most masterly finish with a kind of

Church of San Giorgio de' Schiavoni. Francesco Zucchi, *Teatro delle fabbriche più cospicue in prospettiva, sì pubbliche, che private della città di Venezia* (Venice: 1740), plate 25.

24

universal largeness of feeling, and he who has it well in his memory will never hear the name of Carpaccio without a throb of almost personal affection. Such indeed is the feeling that descends upon you in that wonderful little chapel of St. George of the Slaves, where this most personal and sociable of artists has expressed all the sweetness of his imagination. The place is small and incommodious, the pictures are out of sight and ill-lighted, the custodian is rapacious, the visitors are mutually intolerable, but the shabby little chapel is a palace of art. Mr. Ruskin has written a pamphet about it which is a real aid to enjoyment, though I can't but think the generous artist, with his keen senses and his just feeling, would have suffered to hear his eulogist declare that one of his other productions – in the Museo Civico of Palazzo Correr, a delightful portrait of two Venetian ladies with pet animals – is the "finest picture in the world." It has no need of that to be thought admirable; and what more can a painter desire? (*Venice*, 28)

The painting James mentions was commonly thought to represent St. Jerome in the 19th century, as the other paintings on the same side, representing St. Jerome leading the lion to his monastery and the death of St. Jerome. It is now referred to as St. Augustine. S. Giorgio degli Schiavoni does not mean "of the slaves". Schiavoni are the Dalmatians, faithful subjects of the Venetian Republic, who were partly of Slav origin. As you leave turn right, go over the bridge Ponte de la Comenda, keep going along the Fondamenta and take the third street, Calle S. Lorenzo, on your left (just before the little portico). Follow the calle S. Lorenzo to Campo S. Lorenzo, turn left into the Campo and go over the bridge of S. Lorenzo, down into the Fondamenta S. Lorenzo, first right then left into the Calle Larga S. Lorenzo, and right again under a tiny passageway into Calle Capello (this Palazzo Capello is *not* the one of the *Aspern Papers*). After the bridge turn left along the small Fondamenta S. Giovanni Laterano, at the end turn right into Calle S. Giovanni Laterano, left again along the little Fondamenta and right again taking the Ponte dell'Ospedaletto: walk straight ahead and then turn left. You are in **Campo SS. Giovanni e Paolo**, where you can stand in awe in front of the the **Bartolomeo Colleoni statue** on horseback, by Verrocchio, and think of the narrator of *The Aspern Papers*, descending from his gondola in front of the statue after wandering aimlessly to the Lido, having received the shock of Tina's revelation: he will be able to

have the precious papers if they remain in the family, if the narrator marries her:

> I only know that in the afternoon, when the air was aglow with the sunset, I was standing before the church of Saints John and Paul and looking up at the small

Colleoni's momument near the Church of SS. Giovanni e Paolo. Giovanni Pividor, *Souvenirs de Venise* (Venice: 1836), plate 18.

square-jawed face of Bartolommeo Colleoni, the terrible *condottiere* who sits so sturdily astride his huge bronze horse on the high pedestal on which Venetian gratitude maintains him. The statue is incomparable, the finest of all mounted figures, unless that of Marcus Aurelius, who rides benignant before the Roman Capitol, be finer; but I was not thinking of that; I only found myself staring at the triumphant captain as if he had an oracle on his lips. The western light shines into all his grimness at that hour and makes it wonderfully personal. But he continued to look far over my head, at the red immersion of another day – he had seen so many go down into the lagoon through centuries – and if he were thinking of battles and stratagems they were of a different quality from any I had to tell him of. He couldn't direct me what to do, gaze up at him as I might (*The Aspern Papers,* 295)

The fact that James did not describe at length the interior of the Gothic church of SS. Giovanni e Paolo, where there is a gorgeous Giovanni Bellini altarpiece, might have to do with Ruskin's negative comments on some of the richly carved tombs of the *Dogi*.

Part II. From SS. Giovanni e Paolo to S. Cassiano.

Grimani Theater near Giovanni Grisostomo (Malibran Theater), interior view. Vincenzo Coronelli, *Singolarità di Venezia: I Palazzi* (Venice: ca. 1710).

From Campo SS. Giovanni e Paolo take the Fondamenta Dandolo, go over the Ponte Rosso, into Calle delle Erbe, over the bridge at its end (Ponte delle Erbe), left along the Fondamenta delle Erbe, over the next bridge and into Campo S. Marina; cross it sideways to the right, walk under the sottoportico into Calle Scaleta, walk all along the calle and over the bridge (Ponte Marco Polo) and you are at the back of the **Teatro Malibran**; keep going under the sottoportico into the Corte del Milion and again under the sottoportico del Teatro, on your right, to the front of the theatre, where James refused to go with the Gardners one sweltering evening to hear the opera *Maometto II,* by the Maestro Lorenzi-Fabris, with a libretto by Taddeo Wiel, as he wrote to Mrs. Curtis on July 10, 1892:

> They went (Mrs. Jack and her three friends and Mr. Jack) last night to a première at the Malibran – an opera with libretto by Viel, who had sent boxes and other blandishments. They roasted, I believe, all the more that they frantically applauded – while I met the wandering airs on the lagoon (*Letters III,* 390).

Walk a few steps away from the theatre and you are at the **San Giovanni Crisostomo Church**. Here you can admire the *St. Jerome, St. Christopher and St. Augustine* (1513) by Giovanni Bellini (first chapel on the right) and the *St. John Chrisostomos and the Saints Augustine, John the Baptist, Liberal, Mary Magdalene, Agnes and Catherine* (1509-1511) by Sebastiano dal Piombo, on the main altar:

> There is another noble John Bellini, one of the very few in which there is no Virgin, at San Giovanni Crisostomo – a St. Jerome, in a red dress, sitting aloft upon the rocks and with a landscape of extraordinary purity behind him. The absence of the peculiarly erect Madonna makes it an interesting surprise among the works of the painter and gives it a somewhat less strenuous air. But it has brilliant beauty and the St. Jerome is a delightful old personage.
> The same church contains another great picture for which the haunter of these places must find a shrine apart in his memory; one of the most interesting things he will have seen, if not the most brilliant. Nothing appeals more to him than the three figures of Venetian ladies which occupy the foreground of a smallish canvas of Sebastian del Piombo, placed over the high altar of San Giovanni Crisostomo. Sebastian was a Venetian by birth, but few of his productions are to be seen in his native place; few indeed are to be seen anywhere.

Church of San Giovanni Grisostomo.
Venezia monumentale pittoresca
(Venice: 1865), plate 50.

The picture represents the patron-saint of the church, accompanied by other saints and by the wordly votaries I have mentioned. These ladies stand together on the left, holding in their hands little white caskets; two of them are in profile, but the foremost turns her face to the spectator. This face and figure are almost unique among the beautiful things of Venice, and they leave the susceptible observer with the impression of having made, or rather having missed, a strange, a dangerous, but a most valuable acquaintance. The lady, who is superbly handsome, is the typical Venetian of the sixteenth century, and she remains for the mind the perfect flower of that society. Never was there a greater air of breeding, a deeper expression of tranquil superiority. She walks a goddess – as if she trod without sinking the waves of the Adriatic. It is impossible to conceive a more perfect expression of the aristocratic spirit either in its pride or in its benignity. This magnificent creature is so strong and secure that she is gentle, and so quiet that in comparison all minor assumptions of calmness suggest only a vulgar alarm. But for all this there are depths of possible disorder in her light-coloured eye (*Venice*, 26-27).

If the caskets are not really white, the one in the middle is now visibly a golden vessel, James's description is, as usual, fascinating: look at the lady, who might be Caterina Contarini Morosini, who commissioned the painting, and was buried with her son and husband in this church. Think also of James's similar wonderful imagining of the life of the young man represented in Titian's *Ritratto virile (Portrait of a Man)* in the Pitti at Florence.

Walk out of the main door of the church and turn left along the Salizzada San Canciano toward Rialto, over one bridge (Ponte dell'Olio); after the Salizzada del Fondaco dei Tedeschi (now the Post Office) you will find yourself in Campo S. Bartolomeo where the statue of Goldoni was celebrated by Browning in a sonnet on its inauguration. You are now in **the Rialto area**, where Merton Densher vaguely had rooms, just like James's friend Herbert Pratt.

Walk over the Rialto Bridge, and keep going straight ahead, to the Campo de le Beccarie, leaving to your right the fish market; walk over the bridge de le Beccarie into Calle de le Beccarie, then turn left into Calle dei Boteri and right into Calle del Cristo and into the Campo **S. Cassiano**. Enter the church and look at Tintoretto's *Crucifixion* on the right as you enter from the side door. On September 25 1869, James wrote to his brother about this painting, defining it "the greatest of all", comparing it to the better known huge painting in the Scuola di San Rocco, and referring William to the description given by Ruskin. In *Travelling Companions* he used the painting to emphasize the different reactions of the two young people, describing it however at length. One can find James's own poetics in the description of this painting:

> The little boy arrived with the sacristan and his key, and we were ushered into the presence of Tintoretto's Crucifixion. This great picture is one of the greatest of the Venetian school. Tintoretto, the travelled reader will remember, has painted two masterpieces on this tremendous theme. The larger and more complex work is at the Scuola di San Rocco; the one of which I speak is small, simple, and sublime. It occupies the left side of the narrow choir of the shabby little church which we had entered, and is remarkable as being, with two or three exceptions, the best preserved work of its incomparable author. Never, in the whole range of art, I imagine, has so powerful an effect been produced by means so simple and select; never has the intelligent choice of means to an effect been pursued with such a refinement of perfection. The picture offers to our sight the very central essence of the great tragedy which it depicts. There is no swooning Madonna, no consoling Magdalene, no mockery of contrast, no cruelty of assembled host. We behold the silent summit of Calvary. To the right are the three crosses, that of the Saviour foremost. A ladder pitched against it supports a turbaned executioner, who bends downward to receive the sponge offered him by a comrade. Above the crest of the hill the helmets and spears of a line of soldiery complete the grimness of the scene. The reality of the picture is beyond all words: it is hard to say which is more impressive, the naked horror of the fact represented, or the sensible power of the artist (*Travelling Companions*, 205-6).

Walk back towards Rialto and take a boat either on the same side of the Grand Canal (S. Silvestro) or on the other side (Rialto boatstop).

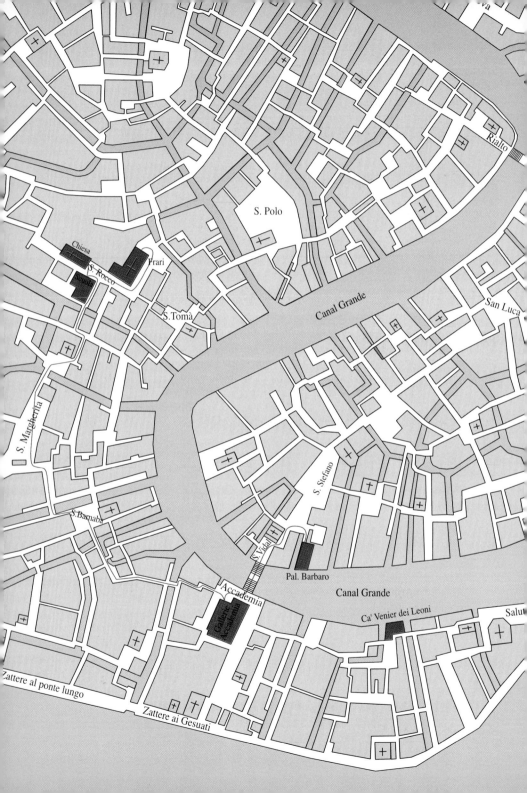

Itinerary 3. From the Palazzo Barbaro to the Scuola di S. Rocco.

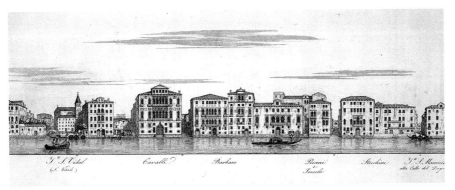

Palazzo Barbaro and adjoining palaces. Antonio Quadri. *Il Canal Grande di Venezia* (Venice: 1828).

Starting point: the **Palazzo Barbaro**'s land entrance, Fondamenta Barbaro 2840, just off Campo S. Stefano (nearest boatstops: S. Angelo or S. M. del Giglio). The land-entrance is at the south end of the Campo S. Stefano, at the end of a small quay, Fondamenta Barbaro, with a cul-de-sac canal, Rio de l'Orso, flowing into the Grand Canal. Look at the Gothic Portal which Ruskin (and James) loved and look up at the corner window on the highest floor: it is the window of the "divine old library" where Mrs. Gardner put a bed for James in 1892 and through which James could hear the voices of the children playing in the Campo, exactly as one does now:

> If in the absence of its masters you have happened to have it [the Palazzo Barbaro] to yourself for twenty-four hours you will never forget the charm of its haunted stillness, late on the summer afternoon for instance, when the call of playing children comes in behind from the campo, nor the way the old ghosts seemed to pass on tip-toe on the marble floors (*The Grand Canal*, 39).

On his 1887 visit James had written:

> I have been paying a long visit - long for me, who likes less and less as I grow older, to stay with people - to the Daniel Curtises, formerly of Boston but who have been living here for years and are the owners of this magnificent old palace – all marble and frescoes and portraits of Doges – a delightful habitation for hot weather (*Letters II*, June 16, 1887,188).

The references to this palace are too many even to try and select a few. The palace was to be James's favorite abode, and the inspiration for the Palazzo Leporelli, the splendid palace where Milly Theale lived what life she had left to live in *The Wings of the Dove*. Even its courtyard, with the grounded gondola, is full of charm, and its wonderful exterior staircase was described by James in one of his *Prefaces*:

… I remember being not long before at work upon it [A London Life], remember in fact beginning it, in one of the wonderful faded back rooms of an old Venetian palace, a room with a pompous Tiepolo ceiling and walls of ancient pale-green damask, slightly shredded and patched, which, on the warm mornings, looked into the shade of a court where a high outer staircase, strikingly bold, yet strikingly relaxed, held together one scarce knew how; where the Gothic windows broke out, on discoloured blanks of wall, at quite arbitrary levels, and where above all the strong Venetian voice, full of history and humanity and waking perpetual echoes, seemed to say more in ten warm words, of whatever tone, than any twenty pages of one's cold pale prose (*Preface* to *The Spoils of Poynton, A London Life, The Chaperon,* 1152)

Walk back towards the Campo, along the small canal, look right to the huge Palazzo Pisani, where William Wetmore Story "was still in time to see in its original place … the splendid Paolo of the National Gallery which appears then to have been known by the charming, if slightly inconsequent, title of the Tent of Darius (*William Wetmore Story and his Friends,* 192), then turn left around the garden gate of the Istituto Veneto di Scienze Lettere ed Arti and into the Campo S. Vidal and to the **Accademia Bridge**. Stand on the bridge turning your back on the Galleries of the Accademia and look to your right: the second palace – after the Franchetti-Cavalli, Gothic but heavily restored in the 19th century – is the Barbaro (made of two buildings). Turn towards the Galleries and look across the Canal to your left: the small house near the unfinished Venier dei Leoni (Peggy Guggenheim Collection) is the **Casa Biondetti**. You can also see the Gothic **Palazzo Semitecolo**, towards the Salute. Walk down the bridge and go the the **Gallerie dell'Accademia** (see Museums, p. 63). Walking out of the Accademia, turn left into Calle Gambara, left into Calle Contarini Corfù, right over the Ponte de le Meravegie, straight ahead into Calle Toletta, right onto Fondamenta della Toletta, over Ponte Lombardo and into Campo S. Barnaba. Cross it towards the Canal, with the colorful fruit and vegetable boat moored nearby, take the first bridge on your right, Ponte dei Pugni, straight into the Rio terrà Canal and left into Campo S. Margherita. Cross the Campo to the right, towards the former church of S. Margherita with the cut-off campanile, over Ponte S. Margherita into Campo S. Pantalon. Turn right into Calle S. Pantalon, left into Calle del Pistor and right into Calle drio la Scuola (Calle behind the Guild of S. Rocco), into Campo S. Rocco. Enter the *Scuola di San Rocco* first, then if you have time go into the church. The *Scuola* is the "temple of the

CHIESA DI Sᵗᵃ MARIA DELLA CARITA'
tie Canonici Regolari

Church of Santa Maria della Carità (Accademia). *Le fabriche, e vedute di Venetia disegnate, poste in prospettiva et intagliate da Luca Carlevarijs* (Venice: 1703), plate 21.

The Church and the School of San Rocco. J.G. Graevius, *Thesaurus antiquitatum et historiarum Italiae* (1722), vol. IX, plate 28.

spirit" of Tintoretto, adored by Ruskin and James, which James – like Ruskin – visited at various times of the day to find the right light (morning light, afternoon light) for the paintings. The lighting is now artificial, and if you can see the paintings better, you don't have the change of natural light which was the norm in the past. However, the restoration of the Scuola and of the paintings fortunately cancelled James's dire prophecy:

> Nothing indeed can well be sadder than the great collection of Tintorets at San Rocco. Incurable blackness is settling fast upon all of them, and they frown at you across the sombre splendour of their great chambers like gaunt twilight phantoms of pictures. To our children's children Tintoret, as things are going, can hardly be more than a name; and such of them as shall miss the tragic beauty, already so dimmed and stained, of the great "Bearing of the Cross" in that temple of his spirit will live and die without knowing the largest eloquence of art (*Venice. An Early Impression,* 59-60).

Fortunately, you *will* be able to experience the stories of the *Annunciation, the Flight into Egypt* etc. on the first floor, and "the tragic beauty" of the huge *Crucifixion* on the second floor. The *Annunciation* (1587) was described by James during his first visit:

> One of his works that has much struck me is a large *Annunciation*, immensely characteristic of this unlikeness to other painters. To the right sits the Virgin, starting back from her angelic visitant with magnificent surprise and terror. The Angel swoops down into the picture, leading a swarm of cherubs, not as in most cases where the subject is treated, as if he had come to pay her a pretty compliment but with a fury characteristic of his tremendous message (*Letters I,* 141)

What struck James immediately in the *Crucifixion* in the Sala dell'Albergo, on the second floor, was Tintoretto's ability to tell many stories in one, huge painting:

> ...in looking at this huge composition you look at many pictures; it has not only a multitude of figures but a wealth of episodes; and you pass from one of these to the other as if you were "doing" a gallery. Surely no single picture in the world contains more of human life; there is everything in it, including the most exquisite beauty. It is one of the

greatest things of art; it is always interesting. There are works of the artist which contain touches more exquisite, revelations of beauty more radiant, but there is no other vision of so intense a reality, an execution so splendid (*Venice,* 21-22).

It was the whole scene that Tintoret seemed to have beheld in a flash of inspiration intense enough to stamp it ineffaceably on his perception; and it was the whole scene, complete, peculiar, individual, unprecedented that he committed to canvas with all the vehemence of his talent.

…

You get from Tintoret's work the impression that he *felt,* pictorially, the great, beautiful, terrible spectacle of human life very much as Shakespeare felt it poetically – with a heart that never ceased to beat a passionate accompaniment to every stroke of his brush (*Venice: An Early Impression,* 59).

You may also like to see the Church of San Rocco (but it is the Scuola which is the great place). Walking out of Scuola di San Rocco walk to the right and you find yourself behind the apse of the **Frari Church**: walk around it and enter the Church. On the main altar you can admire *The Assumption* by Titian, which James found a "magnificent second-rate picture", perhaps following Ruskin's dislike, when he saw it in the Accademia, where the huge painting was transferred between 1816 and 1919. What enchanted James was the (beautiful) Giovanni Bellini triptych on the main altar of **the Sacristy**, at the far end of the right transept, "the treasure of that apartment", *Virgin with Child and Angels Musicians, between Four Saints* (1488). Don't miss it:

There is not a ray in his works of debility or vagueness of conception. In vigor, breadth and richness he is a thorough Venetian. His best pictures here possess an extraordinary perfection. Everything is equal – the full deep beauty of the expression – the masterly – more than masterly firmness and purity of the drawing – and the dimmed, unfathomed lucidity and richness of colour. And then over it all the sort of pious deference has passed and hushed and smoothed and polished till the effect is of unspeakable purity. He has hardly more than one subject – the Virgin and Child, alone, or enthroned and attended with Saints and cherubs; but you will be slow to tire of him, for long after you've had enough of his piety there is food for delight in the secret marvels of his handling (*Letters III,* September 25, 1869, 139).

How is it possible to forget one's visit to the sacristy of the Frari,

CHIESA DE FRARI
Padri Francescani minori Conventuali

The Frari Church. *Le fabriche, e vedute di Venetia disegnate, poste in prospettiva et intagliate da Luca Carlevarijs* (Venice: 1703), plate 23.

34

however frequent they may have been, and the great work of John Bellini which forms the treasure of that apartment?

(…)

Nothing in Venice is more perfect than this, and we know of no work of art more complete. The picture is in three compartments: the Virgin sits in the central division with her child; two venerable saints, standing close together, occupy each of the others. It is impossible to imagine anything more finished or more ripe. It is one of those things that sum up the genius of a painter, the experience of a life, the teaching of a school. It seems painted with molten gems, which have only been clarified by time, and it is as solemn as it is gorgeous and simple as it is deep. Giovanni Bellini is more or less everywhere in Venice, and, wherever he is, almost certain to be first – first, I mean, in his own line: he paints little else than the Madonna and saints; he has not Carpaccio's care for human life at large, nor the Tintoret's nor that of the Veronese. Some of his greater pictures, however, where several figures are clustered together, have a richness of sanctity that is almost profane (*Venice*, 25).

You can go back to boatstop S. Tomà and take a vaporetto there.

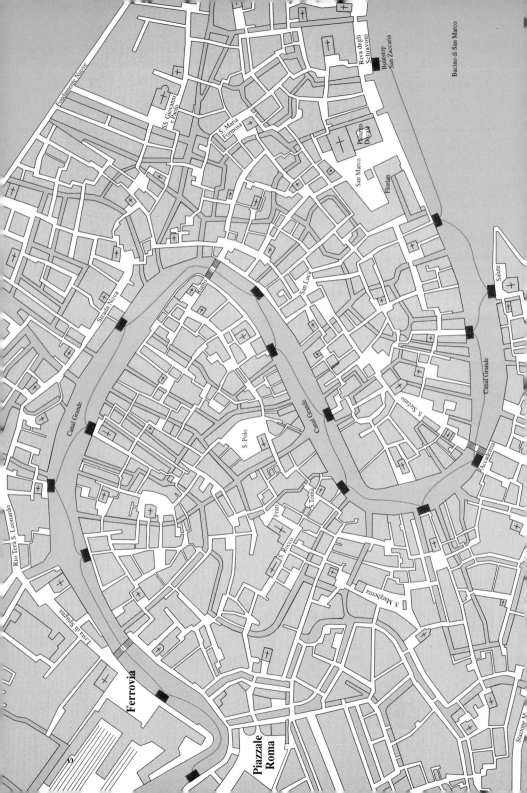

Itinerary 4. The Grand Canal.

Starting point: **Riva degli Schiavoni 4161**, now Pensione Wildner or San Zaccaria boatstops (any: the one for boats n. 20 to S.Servolo or 82 to Tronchetto, near the bridge of La Pietà, or the one nearer St. Mark's). Board **boat n. 1 in front of Hotel Danieli**. If the boat is not crowded (which it mostly is in the summer), sit up front, or stand outside, or sit at the back in the open air and look at *both* sides of the Grand Canal, all the way down to the Station (some vaporetti do not

St. Mark: the Piazzetta. Francesco Zanotto, *Venezia prospettica, monumentale, storica, artistica.* (Venice: 1856), plate 4.

have front seats). Quotations for this itinerary are all taken from the essay *The Grand Canal,* unless a different indication is added.

As the boat approaches the Grand Canal you will see on your left the **Punta della Dogana** (former customhouse) with the golden globe and the figure of Fortune on its top, and on the other side a series of hotels, just as James wrote:

> The charming architectural promontory of the Dogana stretches out the most graceful of arms, balancing in its hand the gilded globe on which revolves the delightful satirical figure of a little weathercock of a woman. This Fortune, this Navigation, or whatever she is called – she surely needs no name – catches the wind in the bit of drapery of which she has divested her rotary bronze loveliness. On the other side of the Canal twinkles and glitters the long row of the happy palaces which are now expensive hotels (33-34).

ALTRA VEDVTA DELLA CHIESA
della Salute

Immediately after, on the same side (left side of the Grand Canal) comes up the great mass of Longhena's **Church of the Salute**, in the Sacristy of which there is a Tintoretto which James loved; use the time during which the boat stops at the Salute to

Church of Santa Maria della Salute. *Le fabriche, e vedute di Venetia disegnate, poste in prospettiva et intagliate da Luca Carlevarijs* (Venice: 1703), plate 5.

look across at **Casa Alvisi**, which is the pink building at the left of Hotel Europa-Regina, and on the right of the Gothic Contarini. It has a sort of terrace on the right, built after James's time. This was the home of Mrs. Bronson, where James stayed in 1887. From the Salute steps you can

> pick straight out of the row a dear little featureless house which, with its pale green shutters, looks straight across at the great door and through the very keyhole, as it were, of the church, and which I needn't call by a name – a pleasant American name – that every one in Venice, these many years, has had on grateful lips. It is the very friendliest house in all the wide world, and it has, as it deserves to have, the most beautiful position. It is a real *porto di mare*, as the gondoliers say – a port within a port; it sees everything that comes and goes, and takes it all in with practised eyes. Not a tint or a hint of the immense iridescence is lost upon it, and there are days of exquisite colour on which it may fancy itself the heart of the wonderful prism. We wave to it from the Salute steps, which we must decidedly leave if we wish to get on, a grateful hand across the water…(35).

> Casa Alvisi is directly opposite the high, broad-based florid church of S. Maria della Salute – so directly that from the balcony over the water-entrance your eye, crossing the canal, seems to find the keyhole of the great door right in a line with it; and there was something in this position that for the time made all Venice-lovers think of the genial *padrona* as thus levying in the most convenient way the toll of curiosity and sympathy (*Casa Alvisi*, 77-78).

At the back of Casa Alvisi there was the **Palazzo Giustiniani Recanati**, where both James and Robert Browning were Mrs. Bronson's guests. The space is now taken up by a modern building.

As the boat moves on, you will see the **Abbazia di San Gregorio**, the first building to the right of the Salute (same side), where there were the Bagni Chitarin (see p. 5), and about six palaces down from it, the Gothic **Palazzo Semitecolo**, which you can identify as the first Gothic palace on the left of the Casa Salviati, which is decorated by a big mosaic. This is the place where Constance Fenimore Cooper committed suicide in 1894. Two palaces down from the Salviati, you will see the **Palazzo Dario**, recognizable by its marble-inlaid facade, with three big round marble decorations, one on each floor:

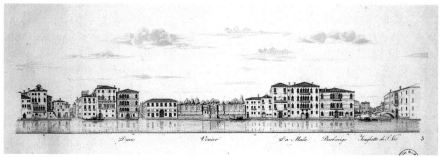

Palazzo Orio-Semitecolo and Palazzo Dario. Antonio Quadri. *Il Canal Grande di Venezia* (Venice: 1828).

Palazzo Corner (Ca' Granda). *Memorie di alcune più celebri fabbriche e situazioni di Venezia* (Venice: 1831) plate 31.

...the delightful little Palazzo Dario, intimately familiar to English and American travellers, picks itself out in the foreshortened brightness. The Dario is covered with the loveliest little marble plates and sculptured circles; it is made up of exquisite pieces – as if there had been only enough to make it small – so that it looks, in its extreme antiquity, a good deal like a house of cards that hold together by a tenure it would be fatal to touch. An old Venetian house dies hard indeed, and I should add that this delicate thing, with submission in every feature, continues to resist the contact of generations of lodgers. It is let out in floors (it used to be let as a whole) and in how many eager hands – for it is in great requisition – under how many fleeting dispensations have we not known and loved it? People are always writing in advance to secure the Jenkins's gondolier, and as the gondola passes we see strange faces at the windows – though it's ten to one we recognise them – and the millionth artist coming forth with his traps at the watergate. The poor little Dario is one of the most flourishing booths at the fair (45-46).

This palace was the house of historian Rawdon Brown from 1838 to 1842.

In the meantime turn to the right side and you will see the enormous pile of the palace **Corner de la Ca' Granda**, built by Jacopo Sansovino (work began in 1533, and the building was not finished in 1556), still the seat of the Prefettura:

> The faces at the window [of Palazzo Dario] look out at the great Sansovino – the splendid pile that is now occupied by the Prefect. I feel decidedly that I don't object as I ought to the palaces of the sixteenth and seventeenth centuries. Their pretensions impose upon me, and the imagination peoples them more freely than it can people the interior of the prime. Was not moreover this masterpiece of Sansovino once occupied by the Venetian post-office, and thereby intimately connected with an ineffaceable first impression of the author of these remarks? He had arrived, wondering, palpitating, twenty-three years ago, after nightfall, and, the first thing on the morrow, had repaired to the post-office for his letters (46).

James clearly reacts to Ruskin's vetoes on this kind of buildings, admitting that he likes it. At the end of the passage he wondered whether he had "misdirected his emotion" in identifying this as the post-office to which he had rushed in 1869. He had. The post-office was the Palazzo Grimani, also on the Grand Canal, near Rialto, built by Sanmicheli, similar in style.

39

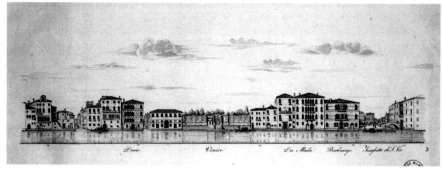

View of the Grand Canal between Palazzo Loredan Balbi-Valier and Palazzo Querini with Casa Biondetti.
Antonio Quadri, *Canal Grande di Venezia* (Venice: 1828), plate 5.

Turn your attention now again to the other side of the Canal where you will identify easily the unfinished Palazzo Venier dai Leoni, now the Peggy Guggenhiem Collection: the first modest house on its right is the **Casa Biondetti**, where James lived and worked as the literary executor of Constance Fenimore Woolson's papers after her suicide in 1894; across the Rio di San Vio, the big **Palazzo Loredan** (now Cini) was the house of Don Carlos, the pretender to the throne of Spain, mentioned by James as a member of Venetian society.

After a big garden, on the same side, the second palace before the bridge of the Accademia is the **Contarini dal Zaffo** (1562-1582), then Manzoni, Angaran, and **at the time Montecuccoli**, now Polignac-Decazes, the palace that Robert Browning almost bought.

> Far-descended and weary, but beautiful in its crooked old age, with its lovely proportions, its delicate round arches, its carvings and disks of marble, is the haunted Montecuculi. Those who have a kindness for Venetian gossip like to remember that it was once for a few months the property of Robert Browning, who, however, never lived in it, and who died in the splendid Rezzonico (42).

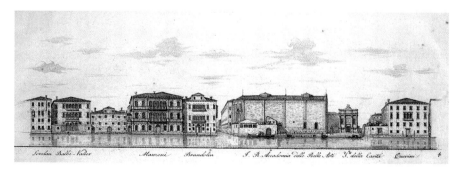

Palazzo Contarini-Dal Zaffo and the Accademia. Antonio Quadri, *Canal Grande di Venezia* (Venice: 1828).

Palazzo Barbaro, lithograph, Giuseppe Moro, from a drawing by Marco Moro. Giovanni Jacopo Fontana, *Venezia Monumentale. I palazzi*, Venezia, 1847.

Across from it, on the opposite side of the Grand Canal, again the second palace before the Accademia Bridge, is the **Palazzo Barbaro** (the windows of the second *piano nobile* are boarded up with planks). It is a palace made of a Gothic one, to the left, and a later one (to the right): the big salon where James had tea was built by architect Antonio Gaspari at the end of the seventeenth century uniting the two buildings. The Palazzo Barbaro balcony provides the recurring point of view in the essay *The Grand Canal*. You can clearly discern the water entrance (to the left, near the small canal), where the Curtises's gondola would drop the Curtises, James, the Gardners, off. The Curtises bought the second *piano nobile* and the upper part of the house in 1885; the first piano nobile and the mezzanino were owned by Countess Pisani, née Evelyn van Millingen, the beautiful woman who, appearing in a box at the Fenice dressed in oriental clothes, at eighteen, conquered and married the last of the Pisani, Almorò. She had been born in Constantinople and educated in Rome. James met her when she was no longer young, and found her still fascinating and beautiful.

Behind the series of windows of the second *piano nobile,* you can imagine Milly Theale, with her "thorough make-believe of a settlement", walking among the stucco-works and the paintings of the great *cameron:*

> Not yet so much as this morning had she felt herself sink into possession; gratefully glad that the warmth of the Southern summer was still in the high florid rooms, palatial chambers where hard cool pavements took reflexions in their lifelong polish, and where the sun on the stirred sea-water, flickering up through the open windows, played over the painted "subjects" in the splendid ceilings – medaillons of purple and brown, of brave old melancholy colour, medals as of old reddened gold, embossed and beribboned, all toned with time and all flourished and scolloped and gilded about (a nest of white cherubs, friendly creatures of the air) and appreciated by the aid of a second tier of smaller lights, straight opening to the front (*The Wings of the Dove*, 260).

Leaving behind the Palazzo Barbaro, you will pass now under the wooden **Accademia Bridge**, which has replaced the "deplorable iron bridge" (1854) of James's time. To your left you can see the **Scuola della Carità and Accademia Galleries** (see p. 63). On the other side of the Canal, the **Palazzetto Falier**, with two covered terraces on the sides, used to be one of the houses where W. D. Howells, the author of *Venetian Life*, a book much appreciated by James, lived for a while. On the opposite side, three palaces

down fom the Accademia, you will see the two palaces **Contarini dagli Scrigni-Corfù**, those Mr. Russell Peabody wanted, according to James, to "knock into one":

> Mr. Peabody-Russell of the U.S. has just bought two Contarini palaces, and is going to "knock them into one"! I tremble for what that one will be (*LPB*, 81, Feb.27,1887).

Fortunately this did not happen.

Across from it the large Palazzo Grassi, in James's time a hotel. On the left side of the Grand Canal, you will see the huge pile of the **Ca' Rezzonico**, begun by Baldassarre Longhena in 1667, one of the palaces Ruskin could not stand as an example of the "Grotesque Renaissance" (after the death of Longhena in 1682, building was continued by A. Gaspari, and finished by Giorgio Massari in 1758). It was bought by Pen Browning in 1888, and decorated with his own pretty awful statues and frescoes. Pen sold it in 1906 after his divorce from his wife Fanny, whose money had bought the palace, all of it. Before the Brownings, the Rezzonico had been used as studios for painters, including John S. Sargent. Robert Browning died there on December 12, 1889. It is now the Museum of 18th century Venice.

> This great seventeenth century pile, throwing itself upon the water with a peculiar florid assurance, a certain upward toss of its cornice which gives it the air of a rearing sea-horse, decorates immensely – and within, as well as without – the wide angle that it commands (42-43).
>
> What Pen Browning has done here, through his American wife's dollars, with the splendid Palazzo Rezzonico, transcends description for the beauty, and, as Ruskin would

Ca' Rezzonico. *Venezia monumentale pittoresca* (Venice, 1865), plate 9.

42

say, "wisdom and rightness" of it. It is altogether royal and imperial – but "Pen" isn't kingly and the *train de vie* remains to be seen. Gondoliers ushering in friends from pensions won't fill it out (*Letters III*, 287, June 6, 1890, to Alice James).

James had initially declared that Pen had filled the Rezzonico with "hideous luxuries". On the same side of the Grand Canal, two buildings away from the Rezzonico, the Gothic Brandolin (also the residence of Howells) is followed by two Gothic palaces. The second, on the Rio Nuovo, is the just-restored **Ca' Foscari**, now the seat of the University of Venice:

> There is a more formal greatness in the high square Gothic Foscari, just below it [the Ca' Rezzonico], one of the noblest creations of the fifteenth century, a masterpiece of symmetry and majesty. Dedicated to-day to official uses – it is the property of the State – it looks conscious of the consideration it enjoys, and is one of the few great houses within our range whose old age strikes us as robust and painless. It is visibly "kept up"; perhaps it is kept up too much; perhaps I am wrong in thinking so well of it. These doubts and fears course rapidly through my mind – I am easily their victim when it is a question of architecture – as they are apt to-day, in Italy, almost anywhere, in the presence of the beautiful, of the desecrated or the neglected. We feel at such moments as if the eye of Mr. Ruskin were upon us; we grow nervous and lose our confidence (43).

Ca' Foscari was sold to the Comune (municipality), not to the state, in 1845. It became the Scuola Superiore di Commercio in 1868, located from 1870 in this palace. After the curve of the Grand Canal, on the right, you will see the **Palazzi Mocenigo**, with a plaque to commemorate Byron's Venetian stay:

> It was not dull, we imagine, for Lord Byron, who lived in the midmost of the three Mocenigo palaces, where the writing-table is still shown at which he gave the rein to his passions (48).

Palazzo Cappello and adjoining palaces. Antonio Quadri, *Canal Grande di Venezia* (Venice: 1828).

You then proceed further towards Rialto, leaving behind the Gothic **Palazzo Garzoni**, practically across from the S. Tomà boatstop, where the antique-dealer Richetti used to have his shop: James may have gone there with Mrs. Gardner. It is, for the time being, the place where this pamphlet came out of, the Department of American Studies of the University of Venice, Ca' Foscari.

On the way to Rialto, to your left, with one side on the Rio di S. Polo and one on the Grand Canal, is **Palazzo Cappello**, in James's time the house where Sir Henry Austen Layard, the diplomat and discoverer of Niniveh, and his wife Enid Guest Layard, lived, with a wonderful collection of paintings, including the *Mahomet II* by Gentile Bellini, now at the National Gallery in London. James was taken for tea to Lady Layard's by Mrs. Curtis, for instance on June 22, 1907, as Lady Layard wrote in her diary. She had met James at the Princess of Montenegro's, in Venice, on June 1, 1887, and had seen him again in London.

Before getting to the Rialto bridge, you can see the huge **Palazzo Grimani**, at the time the post-office James misremembered; three buildings down from it, immediately behind the no.1 vaporetto boatstop Rialto, on the right, the **Palazzo Loredan** is still the Municipio, as in James's time:

> For other observers it [the perspective from the Accademia to Rialto] is sufficiently enlivened by so delightful a creation as the Palazzo Loredan, once a masterpiece and at present the Municipio, not to speak of a variety of other immemorial bits whose beauty still has a degree of freshness. Some of the most touching relics of early Venice are here – for it was here she precariously clustered – peeping out of a submersion more pitiless than the sea. As we approach the Rialto indeed the picture falls off and a comparative commonness suffuses it. There is a wide paved walk on either side of the Canal, on which the waterman – and who in Venice is not a waterman? – is prone to seek repose. I speak of the summer days – it is summer Venice that is the visible Venice. The big tarry barges are drawn up at the *fondamenta,* and the bare-legged boatmen in faded blue cotton, lie asleep on the hot stones (48).

James identifies correctly the **Rialto** (Rivo alto: high bank) as the oldest part of the original city. You continue to the bridge:

> The Bridge of Rialto is a name to conjure with, but, honestly speaking, it is scarcely the gem of the composition. There are of

The Rialto Bridge. *Le fabriche, e vedute di Venetia disegnate, poste in prospettiva et intagliate da Luca Carlevarijs* (Venice: 1703), plate 55.

course two ways of taking it – from the water or from the upper passage, where its small shops and booths abound in Venetian character; but it mainly counts as a feature of the Canal when seen from the gondola or even from the awful *vaporetto*. The great curve of its single arch is much to be commended, especially when, coming from the direction of the railway-station, you see it frame with its sharp compass-line the perfect picture, the reach of the Canal on the other side. But the backs of the little shops make from the water a graceless collective hump, and the inside view is the diverting one. The big arch of the bridge – like the arches of all the bridges – is the waterman's friend in wet weather. The gondolas, when it rains, huddle beside the peopled barges, and the young ladies from the hotels, vaguely fidgeting, complain of the communication of insect life (49).

Past the bridge, on your left, you will see **the fruit and vegetable market**, and if it is early morning you will see what James decribed:

The produce of the islands is discharged there, and the fishmongers announce their presence. All one's senses indeed are vigorously attacked; the whole place is violently hot and bright, all odorous and noisy (49).

Past the bridge and the markets, the next huge palace on your left, past the big **Corner (or Cornaro) della Regina** (la "regina" being Catharine, Queen of Cyprus), before you get to the San Stae boatstop, is the **Ca' Pesaro**, traditionally attributed to Baldassarre Longhena, now the Museum of Modern Art. James liked it, in spite of Ruskin:

I have even a timid kindness for the huge Pesaro, far down the Canal, whose main reproach, more even than the coarseness of its forms, is its swaggering size, its want of consideration for the general picture, which the early examples so reverently respect. The Pesaro is as far out of the frame as a modern hotel, and the Cornaro, close to it, oversteps almost equally the modesty of art. One more thing they and their kindred do, I must add, for which, unfortunately, we can patronise them less. They make even the most elaborate material civilisation of the present day seem woefully shrunken and *bourgeois*, for they simply – I allude to the biggest palaces – can't be lived in as they were intended to be. The modern tenant may take in all the magazines, but he bends not the bow of Achilles. He occupies the place, but he doesn't fill it, and he has guests from the neighbouring inns with ulsters and Baedekers (47).

On the other side the **Ca' d'Oro** is next to boatstop Ca' d'Oro, just as James wrote:

As we go further down we see it [the vaporetto] stopping exactly beneath the glorious windows of the Ca' d'Oro. It has chosen its position well, and who shall gainsay it for having put itself under the protection of the most romantic façade in Europe? The companionship of these objects is a symbol; it expresses supremely the present and the future of Venice. Perfect, in its prime, was the marble Ca' d'Oro, with the noble recesses of its *loggie,* but even then it probably never "met a want", like the successful *vaporetto* (50).

The vaporetti started plying the Grand Canal in 1881. The rest of the trip James described as follows, pausing at the **Vendramin-Calergi**, where the grandson of Charles X of France, the duke of Chambord, lived, and where Richard Wagner died in 1883:

> The rest of the course is a reduced magnificence, in spite of interesting bits, of the battered pomp of the Pesaro and the Cornaro, of the recurrent memories of royalty in exile which cluster about the Palazzo Vendramin Calergi, once the residence of the Comte de Chambord (51).

On the other side the **Fondaco dei Turchi**, "which rears a staring renovated front", actually disfigured by the nineteenth century restorations, was then used to house part of the Correr Collection (now in the Correr Museum in Piazza San Marco):

> Even we ourselves, in the irresistible contagion, are going so fast now that we have only time to note in how clever and costly a fashion the Museo Civico, the old Fondaco dei Turchi, has been reconstructed and restored. It is a glare of white marble without and a series of showy majestic halls within, where a thousand curious mementos and relics of old Venice are gathered and classified (50).

As the boat proceeds past S. Stae, the **Rio di Cannaregio** flows from the right into the Canal Grande, and you will see the apse of the **church of S. Geremia** and observe:

> … that we are passing the mouth of the populous Canareggio, next widest of the water-ways, where the race of Shylock abides, and at the corner of which the big colourless church of San Geremia stands gracefully enough on guard (51).

The boat is now approaching the **Bridge of the Scalzi** (1934), now a stone one, an Austrian iron one from 1858 in James's time. The **Church of the Scalzi** will appear to your right, behind the boatstop Ferrovia, and the **Church of San Simeone Profeta** across from it. The Church of the Scalzi was built on a plan by Longhena (1654) and continued by Giuseppe Sardi (1672-1678):

> The rococo church of the Scalzi is here, all marble and malachite, all a cold, hard glitter and a costly, curly ugliness, and here too, opposite, on the top of its high steps, is San Simeone

Profeta, I won't say immortalised, but unblushingly misrepresented, by the perfidious Canaletto. I shall not stay to unravel the mystery of this prosaic painter's malpractices; he falsified without fancy, and as he apparently transposed at will the objects he reproduced, one is never sure of the particular view that may have constituted his subject. It would look exactly like such and such a place if almost everything were not different. San Simeone Profeta appears to hang there upon the wall; but it is on the wrong side of the Canal and the other elements fail to correspond (51-52).

James did not ever really get to like the eighteenth century, including Canaletto, and, even if he does mention the interior of the Scalzi, which he obviously did not like, he seems not to have even looked at the huge Tiepolo ceiling, which had not yet been destroyed by a bomb (1915) in his time.

The rest of the Grand Canal is not even mentioned by James, as the terminal of Piazzale Roma did not exist.

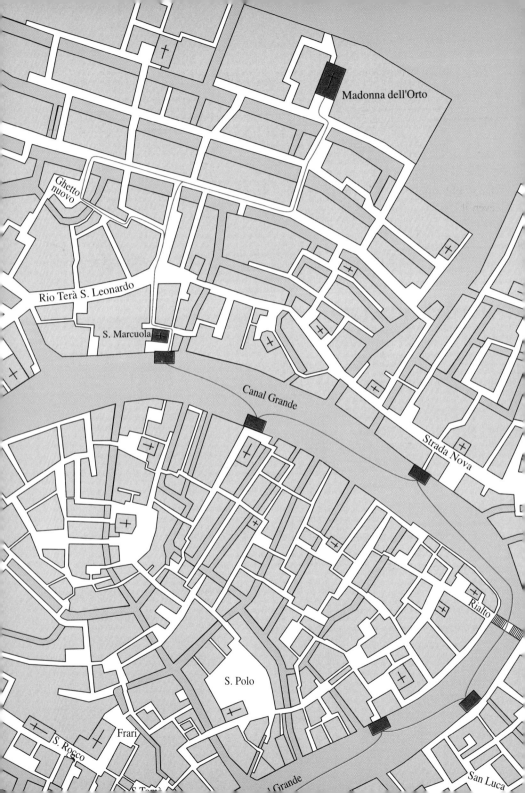

Madonna dell'Orto

Ghetto
nuovo

Rio Terà S. Leonardo

S. Marcuola

Canal Grande

Strada Nova

Rialto

S. Polo

S. Rocco

Frari

San Luca

Itinerary 5. From San Marcuola to the Madonna dell'Orto and the Ghetto.

Madonna dell'Orto church. *Venezia monumentale pittoresca* (Venice, 1865), plate 11.

You can interrupt itinerary 4 at **boatstop San Marcuola**. Walk straight ahead from the boatstop, turn left along the side of the church and right into Rio Terrà del Cristo, continue straight ahead into the Rio Terrà Favretti, over the Ponte Ca' Loredan, right onto the Fondamenta degli Ormesini, and take the first street to your left, Calle del Forno. Walk all the way down to the Ponte del Forno, turn right on the Fondamenta della Sensa, take the first street to your left, Calle Loredan, continue over the Ponte Loredan, and you will see the big church of **Madonna dell'Orto**.

In the Church admire the various paintings by Tintoretto which James loved, in particular the *Presentation of the Virgin* (1552):

> To compare his [Tintoretto's] Presentation of the Virgin, at the Madonna dell'Orto, with Titian's at the Academy, or his [Tintoretto's] Annunciation with Titian's close at hand, is to measure the essential difference between observation and imagination (*Venice: An Early Impression,* 59).

The other famous works by Tintoretto in the church are the *Adoration of the Golden Calf* and *The Day of Doom,* and on the organ doors *The Martyrdom of St. Christopher* and *The Apparition of the Cross.*

On the way out of the church you can walk to **the Ghetto**, "where the race of Shylock abides", and then take one of the boats circling the city at Rio di Cannaregio. The Ghetto was a very poor area of the city, where poor non-Jewish people started living at the end of the 1860s because of low rents. It was one of the area unfrequented by wealthy people.

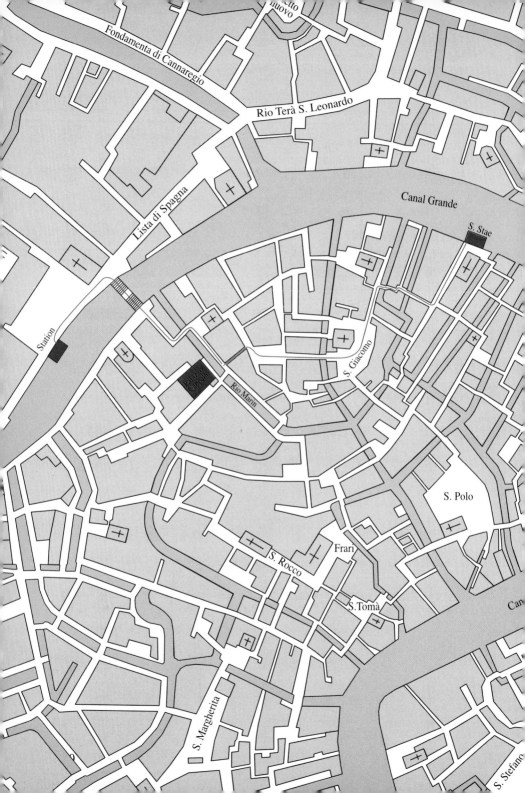

Itinerary 6. *From the Station to the Palazzo Cappello in Rio Marin.*

This is the walk to the **Palazzo Soranzo Cappello in Rio Marin** (end of the 16th, beginning of the 17th century), the palace that James "had more or less in mind", as he wrote to photographer Alvin Langdon Coburn in 1906, when Coburn was to take pictures for the New York Edition of James's novels. The Palazzo Cappello in James's time was where Constance Fletcher (1858-1938) lived, "at periods (with her infirm old mother and her mother's second husband, Eugene Benson)". Miss Fletcher was the author of a very successful novel, *Kismet, a Nile Novel* (1877), published with the pseudonym George Fleming. Her mother had eloped when Constance was nine, with her and her brother's tutor, a painter, Eugene Benson (1839-1908). Constance had gone with them. Benson exhibited several times at the Venice Biennale.

You can either walk through labyrinthine alleys **from Rialto or boatstop S.Stae**, or find your way easily from the station boatstop, both jamesian routes:

> Your best way to get to the Rio Marin will be to obtain guidance, for a few coppers, from some alert Venetian street-boy (or of course you can go, romantically, in a gondola). But the extremely tortuous and complicated walk – taking Piazza San Marco as a starting point – will show you so much, so many bits and odds and ends, such a revel of Venetian picturesqueness, that I advise you doing it on foot as much as possible. You go almost as if you were going to the Station to come out at the end of the bridge opposite the same. Now that I think of it indeed your best way, for shortness, will be to go by Vaporetto, or little steamboat, which plies every few minutes on the Grand Canal, straight to the Stazione, and there crossing the big contiguous iron bridge, walk to the Rio Marin in three or four minutes. It is the old faded, battered-looking, and quite homely and plain (as things go in Venice) old Palazzino on the right of the small Canal, a little way along, as you enter it by the end of the Canal towards the Station. It has a garden behind it, and I think, though I am not sure, some bit of a garden-wall beside it; it doesn't moreover bathe its steps, if I remember right, directly in the Canal, but has a small paved Riva or footway in front of it, and *then* water-steps down from this little quay (*Letters, IV,* 426-7).

James remembered exactly the position of the fondamenta and the riva of the palace. Of course the station bridge is now a stone one, not an iron bridge. If you decide to follow James's instructions, going on foot, and starting perhaps from Rialto rather than San Marco, just follow the signs and arrows to "Ferrovia" (Railway station), always following the arrows to the right when the sign has arrows pointing both to the right and the left. If you decide to take the easier way, from the vaporetto stop of the Station: cross the Grand Canal bridge (Ponte degli Scalzi), walk straight ahead into the Calle Longa, then left into Calle Bergama and over the iron bridge (Ponte Bergama), and you will find yourself on the Fondamenta dei Garzoti, facing the **Palazzo Cappello**, now not at all dilapidated, but the restored seat of the offices of the Sovrintendenza ai Beni Artistici del Veneto. You will see it there:

View of the Palazzo Soranzo-Cappello seen from the water. Vincenzo Coronelli, *Singolarità di Venezia. I Palazzi* (Venice: ca. 1710), plate 176.

The gondola stopped, the old palace was there; it was a house of the class which in Venice carries even in extreme dilapidation the dignified name. "How charming! It's grey and pink!" my companion exclaimed; and that is the most comprehensive description of it. It was not particularly old, only two or three centuries; and it had an air not so much of decay as of quiet discouragement, as if it had rather missed its career. But its wide front, with a stone balcony from end to end of the *piano nobile* or most important floor, was architectural enough, with the aid of various pilasters and arches; and the stucco with which in the intervals it had long ago been endued was rosy in the April afternoon. It overlooked a clean, melancholy, rather lonely canal, which had a narrow *riva* or convenient footway on either side (*The Aspern Papers,* 169).

The **garden** can be seen on the right of the palazzo, and at the back; in James's time it used to be much, much bigger, stretching all the way to the Church of San Simeon Grando. The 20th century housing project by the famous architect Giuseppe Samonà has taken up quite a lot of the garden.
Walk back to Rialto or take a boat at the Station.

View of the Palazzo Soranzo-Cappello seen from the garden. Vincenzo Coronelli, *Singolarità di Venezia. I Palazzi* (Venice: ca. 1710), plate 176.

TRIPS:
To the Islands.

Itinerary 7. To the Lido.

Starting point: any boat (n.1, 82, 51) from the Riva degli Schiavoni.

As we mentioned **the Lido** changed enormously even in James's lifetime. From the early 80s bathing facilities started to become popular, and in the course of the 90s, and later, the whole of the Lido was totally built up. In his first 1869 visit James enjoyed it as a kind of solitary Newport. People used to go to the Lido in a gondola: Browning did so regularly in the Curtises' gondola, the Evanses of *Travelling Companions* also did so, and of course the distraught narrator of *The Aspern Papers* does so towards the end of the story:

> At last, I became conscious that we were near the Lido, far up, on the right hand, as you turn your back to Venice, and I made him put me ashore. I wanted to walk, to move, to shed some of my bewilderment. I crossed the narrow strip and got to the sea-beach – I took my way toward Malamocco. But presently I flung mysef down again on the warm sand, in the breeze, on the coarse, dry grass (*The Aspern Papers,* 292-3).

You will not be put ashore near Malamocco, taking any boat from Riva degli Schiavoni. You will land at S. M. Elisabetta, from which a no longer "rough lane" – but rather a "third rate boulevard" - takes you to the sea: at the far end you will find beaches both to the right (the Des Bains of Thomas Mann's *Death in Venice,* the Excelsior further on), and to the left (less elegant but perfectly pleasant). The Lido has practically lost its identity as an island of sand dunes and orchards: a little of this can still be found near Malamocco (bus or bike), where there is also a lovely church and a small village:

> Along a narrow line in the middle of the island are market-gardens and breeze-twisted orchards, and a hint of hedges and lanes and inland greenery (*Travelling Companions,* 200).

James found it spoiled after his first visit:

> You go to the Lido, though the Lido has been spoiled. When I first saw it, in 1869, it was a very natural place, and there was but a rough lane across the little island from the landing-place to the beach. There was a bathing-place in those days, and a restaurant, which was very bad, but where in the warm evening your dinner didn't much matter as you sat letting it cool on the wooden terrace that stretched out into the sea. To-day the Lido is a part of united Italy and has been made the victim of villanous improvements. A little cockney village has sprung up on its rural bosom and a third-rate boulevard leads from Santa Elisabetta to the Adriatic. There are bitumen walks and gas-lamps, lodging-houses, shops and a *teatro diurno* (*Venice,* 28).

You might like to visit the ancient Jewish cemetery, where Miss Evans and Mr. Brooke went on their own, having left Miss Evans's father at the trattoria with his chance-met old friend. The fortifications are the ones of San Niccolò, at the northern tip of the Lido:

> At one end is a series of low fortifications duly embanked and moated and sentinelled. Still beyond these, half over-drifted with sand and over-clambered rank grasses and coarse thick shrubbery, are certain quaintly lettered funereal slabs, tombs of former Jews of Venice (*Travelling Companions*, 200).

The ancient Jewish cemetery is now surrounded by walls, and no longer spreading out onto the dunes, but the slabs lettered with the Jewish alphabet are still there.

Going to the beach, you will find that it is no longer "lonely and beautiful", but the return to Venice at sunset may be just as striking as in James's time:

> The return to Venice in the sunset is classical and indispensable, and those who at that glowing hour have floated toward the towers that rise out of the lagoon will not easily part with the impression (*Venice*, 29).

> There is no Venice like the Venice of that magical hour. For that brief period her ancient glory returns. The sky arches over her like a vast imperial canopy crowded with its clustering mysteries of light. Her whole aspect is one of unspotted splendor. No other city takes the crimson evanescence of day with such magnificent effect. The lagoon is sheeted with a carpet of fire. All torpid, pallid hues of marble are transmuted into a golden glow. The dead Venetian tone brightens up and quickens into life and lustre, and the spectator's enchanted vision seems to rest on an embodied dream of the great painter who wrought his immortal reveries into the ceilings of the Ducal Palace (*Travelling Companions*, 204).

On the way back from the Lido, James surely had a knowledgeable look at **the island of the Armenians**, the first on the left as you "float" back to Venice, famous for its Byron memories; and to **the island of S. Servolo**, the second on your left, where Shelley's Julian and Maddalo listened to the passionate love story of the madman.

Itinerary 8. To Torcello and Burano.

There are two ways to go to Torcello: in the Summer there are boats from Riva degli Schiavoni, but your best way is to take a boat **from Fondamente Nuove**, on the northern side of the city. Avoid (expensive) package tours that allow you little time on the islands.

James certainly saw Torcello in the light of Ruskin's descriptions, seeing it first in its charming desolation, and later a little bit restored. He also went there with his sister Alice in 1872. Torcello, if you don't get to the island with a mass of tourists, maintains all of its charm, and the Locanda Cipriani of Hemingway's time still has a beautiful garden, full of pomegranates and flowers, looking onto the cathedral, which James would have loved.

> A delicious stillness covered the little campo at Torcello… There was no life but the visible tremor of the brilliant air and the cries of half-a-dozen young children who dogged our steps and clamoured for coppers… (*Venice: An Early Impression*, 55)

The vision of the little urchins, and of a "little unlettered Eros of the Adriatic strand" is pure Ruskin, and should be read entirely.

> Without making this excursion you can hardly pretend to know Venice or to sympathise with that longing for pure radiance which animated her great colourists. It is a perfect bath of light, and I couldn't get rid of a fancy that we were cleaving the upper atmosphere on some hurrying cloud-skiff. At Torcello there is nothing but the light to see – nothing at least but a sort of blooming sand-bar intersected by a single narrow creek which does duty as a canal and occupied by a meagre cluster of huts the dwellings apparently of market-gardeners and fishermen, and by a ruinous church of the eleventh century. It is impossible to imagine a more penetrating case of unheeded collapse. Torcello was the mother-city of Venice, and she lies there now, a mere mouldering vestige, like a group of weather-bleached parental bones left impiously unburied. I stopped my gondola at the mouth of the shallow inlet and walked along the grass beside a hedge to the low-browed, crumbling cathedral. The charm of certain vacant grassy spaces, in Italy, overfrowned by masses of brickwork that are honeycombed by the suns of centuries, is something that I hereby renounce once for all the attempt to express; but you may be sure that whenever I mention such a spot enchantment lurks in it (*Venice: An Early Impression*, 55).

The Cathedral has been restored, and the solitude of the island is difficult to find, full as the grassy campo is of tourists and Venetian lace-work from Honk Kong. But you may still be lucky and be able to enjoy the real beauty of the place.

Then James takes you into the church:

> The church, admirably primitive and curious, reminded me of the two or three oldest churches of Rome – St. Clement and St. Agnes. The interior is rich in grimly mystical

mosaics of the twelfth century and the patchwork of precious fragments in the pavement not inferior to that of St. Mark's. But the terribly distinct Apostles are ranged against their dead gold backgrounds as stiffly as grenadiers presenting arms – intensely personal sentinels of a personal Deity. Their stony stare seems to wait forever vainly for some visible revival of primitive orthodoxy, and one may well wonder whether it finds much beguilement in idly-gazing troops of Western heretics – passionless even in their heresy (*Venice: An Early Impression*, 56-57).

If you don't see Torcello with crowds of tourists, you can still savour its very special atmosphere, and on the way back, after stopping for a walk in **Burano**, a colorful village, enjoy the beauty of the lagoon.

Itinerary 9. To Chioggia.

In the Summer there is a direct boat **from Riva degli Schiavoni to Chioggia**; otherwise take a boat to the Lido, then bus n.11, which rushes you all the way along the thin strip of the Lido, onto a ferry boat at the port of Malamocco, back on the road on the strip of land named Pellestrina, and at the end of the island another boat will take you to Chioggia.

James's mythicizing description of the inhabitants of Chioggia is no longer applicable, you can only see these characters in nineteenth century paintings. You are likely to see miniskirts and blue-jeans all around. However, even if Chioggia is no longer characterized by "hovels", it is still very picturesque, and you can still see fishermen mending their nets, although fishing boats no longer have sails but only motors:

> Chioggia is a larger Burano, and you carry away from either place a half-sad, half-cynical, but altogether pictorial impression of bright-coloured hovels, of bathing in stagnant canals, of young girls with faces of a delicate shape and a susceptible expression, with splendid heads of hair and complexions smeared with powder, faded yellow shawls that hang like old Greek draperies, and little wooden shoes that click as they go up and down the steps of the convex bridges; of brown-cheeked matrons with lustrous tresses and high tempers, massive throats encased with gold beads, and eyes that meet your own with a certain traditional defiance. The men throughout the islands of Venice are almost as handsome as the women; I have never seen so many good-looking rascals. At Burano and Chioggia they sit mending their nets, or lounge at the street corners, where conversation is always high-pitched, or clamour to you to take a boat; and everywhere they decorate the scene with their splendid colour – cheeks and throats as richly brown as the sails of their fishing-smacks – their sea-faded tatters which are always a "costume", their soft Venetian jargon, and the gallantry with which they wear their hats, an article that nowhere sits so well as on a mass of dense Venetian curls (*Venice,* 29-30).

If you have an ear for dialects, you will still hear the peculiar cadence of the "soft" Chioggia jargon, quite detectable even now.

You can have very good fried or grilled fish in Chioggia.

To the Mainland:

Itinerary 10. To Castelfranco and Asolo, back via Treviso.

James and his friends and acquaintances often went to Asolo, the beautiful small town near **Castelfranco**, Giorgione's birthplace (the *Pala di Castelfranco* is temporarily at the Accademia Galleries in Venice). You can take a train to Castelfranco and then go by taxi to **Asolo**, where the exiled Catharine, Queen of Cyprus, held court. If you drive, the road is always full of traffic. On the way back you can travel by bus to Treviso, walk around the centre of this beautiful city, and then take the train to Venice.

The main reason why James and his friends went to Asolo was to see Mrs. Bronson, who bought a house, La Mura, as a sort of homage to Robert Browning, whose poem *Pippa Passes,* set in Asolo, she loved. Browning also went to Asolo to see Mrs. Bronson, and his son Pen bought a house there and lived there for a number of years.

Asolo is a perfectly preserved small town, and although the countryside all around is blighted by small businesses and factories, the Asolo area is miraculously still very beautiful. James wrote to florentine dr. Baldwin in 1890:

> On Tuesday 24th I jog back over the Brenner, in five hours, to Botzen, whence on Wednesday, if all goes well, I take an Einspaenner and drive (for two days) back into blessed Italy, to *Asolo,* where I spend a couple of days with Mrs. Bronson, who, as perhaps you know, has a little house there. (Asolo is in the sweet Venetian hills, near Bassano, and Pen Browning, the other day in Venice, recommended highly to take the drive in question – from Botzen to Bassano, by Primiero and San Martino, other beautiful Dolomites.) (*Letters III,* 292, 20 June 1890, to dr. Baldwin).

An Einspaenner was a one-horse carriage, and Pen Browning was totally right in advising the still beautiful journey over the Dolomites, in particular San Martino, where many of the Anglo-Venetians went to escape the summer heat.

On June 1894, from Casa Biondetti, James wrote to Mrs. Gardner:

> Dearest Mrs. Gardner.
> I tried to write to you yesterday from Asolo – for *auld lang syne,* but the "view" got so between me and my paper that I couldn't get round the purple mountains to dip my pen. I have just been spending three days with Mrs. Bronson – alone with her and Edith. Three days of great loveliness (*Cara Donna Isabella,* 122).

In the essay on Mrs. Bronson and Casa Alvisi, James could not fail to refer to Asolo:

> At Asolo, periodically, the link with Browning was more confirmed than weakened, and there, in old Venetian territory, and with the invasion of visitors comparatively checked, her [Mrs. Bronson's] preferentially small house became again a setting for the pleasure of talk

and the sense of Italy. It contained again its small treasures, all in the pleasant key of the homelier Venetian spirit. The plain beneath it stretched away like a purple sea from the lower cliffs of the hills, and the white *campanili* of the villages, as one was perpetually saying, showed on the expanse as scattered sails of ships. The rumbling carriage, the old-time, rattling, red-velveted carriage of provincial, rural Italy, delightful and quaint, did the office of the gondola; to Bassano, to Treviso, to high-walled Castelfranco, all pink and gold, the home of Giorgione (*Casa Alvisi,* 81-82).

Walk along the Via Browning, from the central piazza, and on your right, at its end, you will see La Mura, so called because it was built on the walls of Asolo:

> Here, beside the "gate" where our friends [the Storys] had seen their last of Browning, also a visitor tenderly protected by her [Mrs. Bronson], she [Mrs. Bronson] had established one of the quaintest possible little places of *villeggiatura* - the gate being the empty arch of one of the old town entrances, a barrier long since humbly removed, to match with all other humilities, and the house itself resting half upon the dismantled, dissimulated town-wall. No sweeter spot, in all the sweetness of Italy, could have offered itself to old Italianised friends for confident renewals and unwitting farewells (*William Wetmore Story and his Friends,* 282-3).

Asolo has a small museum, with paintings by Eugene Benson, Constance Fletcher's step-father, and mementoes of Eleonora Duse. You can have a look at the theatre, where Mrs. Bronson staged her plays, or *commediette, Son Paron Mi* and *Un inglese a Venezia la Vigilia de S. Martin,* in perfect Venetian dialect, on February 2, 1896.
Near Asolo (by taxi), is the Villa Maser, built by Palladio and frescoed by Veronese, a villa that none of our nineteenth century friends seems to have visited or written about.

Itinerary 11. To Padua.

Padua can be reached by train or bus from Piazzale Roma; buses and trains run very often (every half hour or so). From the railway station or bus station you can take a bus or taxi to the church of St. Anthony, the patron saint of the city, but the highlight of your visit, as for Miss Evans and Mr. Brooke, will be the Cappella degli Scrovegni, with the Giotto cycle of frescoes, recently restored. You will no longer find in the Cappella degli Scrovegni the shabbiness that made it so attractive to the narrator of *Travelling Companions,* as the Chapel is now part of a museum system, but the beauty of Giotto's "little compartments" is all there for you to enjoy:

> I have no space and little power to enumerate and describe the various curiosities of Padua. I think we saw them all. We left the best, however, for the last, and repaired in the late afternoon, after dining fraternally at a restaurant, to the Chapel of Giotto. This little empty church, standing unshaded and forlorn in the homely market-garden which was once a Roman arena, offers one of the deepest lessons of Italian travel. Its four walls are covered, almost from base to ceiling, with that wonderful series of dramatic paintings which usher in the golden prime of Italian art. I had been so ill-informed as to fancy that to talk about Giotto was to make more or less a fool on one's self, and that he was the especial property of the mere sentimentalists of criticism. But you no sooner cross the threshold of that little ruinous temple – a mere empty shell, but coated as with the priceless substance of fine pearls and vocal with a murmured eloquence as from the infinite of art – than you perceive with whom you have to deal: a complete painter of the very strongest sort. In one respect, assuredly, Giotto has never been surpassed – in the art of presenting a story. The amount of dramatic expression compressed into those quaint little scenic squares would equip a thousand later masters. How, beside him, they seem to fumble and grope and trifle! And he, beside them, how direct he seems, how essential, how masculine! What a solid simplicity, what an immediate purity and grace! The exhibition suggested to my friend and me more wise reflections than we had skill to utter. "Happy, happy art," we said, as we seemed to see it beneath Giotto's hand tremble and thrill and sparkle, almost, with a presentiment of its immense career, "for the next two hundred years what a felicity will be yours!" The chapel door stood open into the sunny corn-field, and the lazy litter of verdure enclosed by the crumbling oval of Roman masonry. A loutish boy who had come with the key lounged on a bench, awaiting tribute, and gazing at us as we gazed. The ample light flooded the inner precinct, and lay hot upon the coarse, pale surface of the painted wall. There seemed an irresistible pathos in such a combination of shabbiness and beauty... We went over the little compartments one by one: we lingered and returned and compared... At last the light began to fade and the little saintly figures to grow quaint and terrible in the gathering dusk (*Travelling Companions,* 209-210).

Mr. Brooke echoes James's own words of October 6, 1869, to his sister Alice:

> I have always fancied that to say anything about Giotto was to make more or less a fool of one's self and that he was the especial property of the mere sentimentalists of criticism. But

he is a real complete painter of the very strongest sort. In one respect he has never been surpassed – in the faculty of telling a story – the mastery of dramatic representation. The amount of dramatic expression pressed into these quaint little squares would equip a hundred later masters. And then the simplicity – the purity – the grace! The whole exhibition suggests more reflections than I have time for. Happy, happy art, you say to yourself as you seem to see it, beneath Giotto's hand, tremble and thrill with a presentiment of its immense career for the next two hundred year (*Letters I,* 146).

You can then walk back to the central area of the city, which is now pedestrianized, and have a drink at famous Caffè Pedrocchi, just like James's characters.

MUSEUMS

You *must* visit separately:
Gallerie dell'Accademia, Scuola di San Rocco, Museo Correr (this is now located at the end of Piazza San Marco; as mentioned, in James's time it was at the Fondaco dei Turchi, now the Museum of Natural History, on the Grand Canal), Palazzo Ducale. Of the churches not mentioned in the itineraries you must visit the Church of San Giorgio Maggiore (on the island) and the Salute Church and its Sacristy.

Gallerie dell'Accademia: the basic thing to remember is that the museum looked very different during all of James's visits, mainly due to the fact the paintings were in different rooms and that the *Assumption (Assunta)* by Titian was from 1816 to 1919 in the Accademia (room 1 from 1816 to 1886, and room 2 from 1886 to 1919), and not in the Frari church. The paintings named by James were also hung in different rooms. You enter room 1 (sala I), where you meet the golden background "primitives", which James did not particularly ever like, if he remembered being taken to see some "worm-eaten dyptichs and tryptichs, of angular saints and seraphs, of black Madonnas and obscure Bambinos" (*Autobiography*, 152), in New York, as a little boy. Rooms II, III, IV, V offer a wealth of Giovanni Bellini Madonnas and other wonderful *pale* (altarpieces), together with famous paintings by Giorgione. In Room VI you will find the *Adam and Eve*, the *Abel and Cain* so admired by James, together with other works by Tintoretto. In Room VII a whole side of the hall is taken up by the *Convito in Casa Levi* by Veronese, a painting that together with the Louvre *Marriage of Cana* acted in various ways on James's imagination in his novels, stories, autobiography, and in *The American Scene*. In the same room you can see a series of big Tintoretto paintings, among them the *Miracle of St. Mark's*, one of the most famous ones also in the 19th century, close to the *Stealing of the Body of St. Mark's*, to *St. Mark saving a Saracen,* and to *St. Mark's Rest.* None is now "atrociously hung - away aloft in the air."
James's first reaction to these paintings is recorded in a letter to his brother William, written on his first visit to Venice in 1869 (September 25th):

> His *Miracle of St. Mark's* is a tremendous work, with life enough in it to animate a planet. They can all paint a crowd and this is as much Venetian as individual. A better specimen of his peculiar power is a simple *Adam and Eve,* in the same room as a *Cain and Abel,* its mate, both atrociously hung – away aloft in the air. Adam sits on a bank with his back to you; Eve facing you, with one arm wound round a tree leans forward and holds out an apple. The composition is so simple that it hardly exists and yet the painting is so rich and expressive that it seems as if the *natural,* the real, could go no further – unless indeed in the other, where Cain assaults Abel with an intent to kill more murderous and tragical than words can describe it (*Letters I,* 141).

On the opposite wall admire the *Pietà* by Titian and the *Annunciation* by Veronese. Proceed to Room XIII where there are several more portraits and paintings by Tintoretto, ignore – if you keep in a Jamesian mood - the 18th century paintings in the wide corridor, and after looking at the *Pala di Castelfranco* by Giorgione in Room XXIII, move to Room XX, where you will find the wonderful cycle of the *Procession* and the *Miracle of the Cross at San Lorenzo* by Gentile Bellini, and *The Miracle of the Cross at Rialto* by Vittor Carpaccio; proceed to Room XXI where you can admire the *Stories of St. Ursula* by Carpaccio, beloved by Ruskin, who saw in young Ursula's features those of Rose La Touche, and beloved by James and Edith Wharton.

In the last room, the Sala dell'Albergo della Scuola della Carità, you will see the wonderful *Presentation of the Virgin* by Titian, which James did not like so much. The painting is now in its original location, but James did not see it here as it was transferred in 1828 to one of the new rooms (now room 10), where it remained until 1895.

Scuola di San Rocco (see p. 33): it is almost impossible to quote a short excerpt from James's letters or essays on the paintings in these halls:

> Solemn indeed is the place, solemn and strangely suggestive, for the simple reason that we shall scarcely find four walls elsewhere that inclose within a like area an equal quantity of genius. The air is thick with it and dense and difficult to breathe… (*Venice*, 22).

Museo Correr: don't miss the so called *Le cortigiane* (The courtesans) by Vittor Carpaccio now in the Quadreria of the Correr (second floor). James saw it in the Fondaco dei Turchi. The painting is now called *L'attesa. Caccia in laguna*, or *Le due dame*:

> .. a delightful portrait of two Venetian ladies with pet animals (*Venice*, 28)

It has recently been recognized that this painting is the lower part of a larger painting, the upper part of which, a lagoon hunting scene, is in the J. Paul Getty Museum (California).

Palazzo Ducale (see pp. 16-17): this was the light and serene place that James contrasted with the dark and tragic aura of the Scuola di San Rocco:

> All the history of Venice, all its splendid stately past, glows around you in a strong sea-light. Every one here is magnificent, but the great Veronese is the most magnificent of all. He swims before you in a silver cloud; he thrones in an eternal morning. The deep blue sky burns behind him, streaked across with milky bars; the white colonnades sustain the richest canopies, under which the first gentlemen and ladies in the world both render homage and receive it. Their glorious garments rustle in the air of the sea and their sun-lighted faces are the very complexion of Venice. The mixture of pride and piety, of politics and religion, of art and patriotism, gives a splendid dignity to every scene. Never was a painter more nobly joyous, never did an artist take a greater delight in life, seeing it all as a kind of breezy festival and feeling it through the medium of perpetual success. He revels in the gold-framed ovals of the ceilings, multiplies himself there with the fluttering movement of an embroidered banner that tosses itself into the blue (*Venice*, 23).

The essence of the Venetian Republic is all there, in James's description.
Take time to wonder around and back, to see your – and James's - favourite pictures.

San Giorgio Maggiore: don't miss *The Last Supper* by Tintoretto in the church:

> Compare his "Last Supper" at San Giorgio – its long, diagonally placed table, its dusky
> spaciousness, its scattered lamp-light and halo-light, its startled, gesticulating figures, its
> richly realistic foreground – with the customary formal, almost mathematical rendering of
> the subject, in which impressiveness seems to have been sought in elimination rather than
> comprehension (*Venice: An Early Impression,* 59).

Church of the Salute and Sacristy:
James did not really like the interior of the church, "the big white church of Longhena –
an empty shaft beneath a perfunctory dome", but he adored the *Marriage Feast of Cana,*
in the Sacristy, about which he wrote in 1892:

> "The Marriage in Cana," at the Salute, has all his characteristic and fascinating
> unexpectedness – the sacrifice of the figure of our Lord, who is reduced to the mere final
> point of a clever perspective, and the free, joyous presentation of all the other elements of
> the feast. Why, in spite of this queer one-sidedness, does the picture give us no impression
> of a lack of what the critics call reverence? For no other reason that I can think of than
> because it happens to be the work of its author, in whose very mistakes there is a singular
> wisdom. Mr. Ruskin has spoken with sufficient eloquence of the serious loveliness of the
> row of heads of the women on the right, who talk to each other as they sit at the
> foreshortened banquet. There could be no better example of the roving independence of
> the painter's vision, a real spirit of adventure for which his subject was always a cluster of
> accidents; not an obvious order, but a sort of peopled and agitated chapter of life, in which
> the figures are submissive pictorial notes. These notes are all there in their beauty and
> heterogeneity, and if the abundance is of a kind to make the principle of selection seem in
> comparison timid, yet the sense of "composition" in the spectator – if it happen to exist –
> reaches out to the painter in peculiar sympathy (*The Grand Canal,* 36).

Ruskin's observations in the *Venetian Index* had been the following:

> The spectator looks all along the table, at the farther end of which are seated Christ and the
> Madonna, the marriage guests on each side of it, on one side men, on the other women;
> the men are set with their backs to the light, which, passing over their heads and glancing
> slightly at the tablecloth, falls in full length along the line of young Venetian women, who
> thus fill the whole centre of the picture with one broad sunbeam, made up of fair faces and
> golden hair (*The Stones of Venice,* III, 356).

The Festa del Redentore.

As we mentioned, the Feast of the Redeemer is still a very popular feast, taking place on the third Saturday in July, when a bridge made of barges is built across the Canale della Giudecca, between the Zattere and the Church of the Redentore. It celebrates the ceasing of the plague, when the Venetian Senate decided to build a church to the Redeemer for freeing the city from the plague (1576). A solemn procession inaugurates the bridge, with the Patriarch of Venice leading it and all the civil and religious authorities taking part.

In James's times people would go out to the Giudecca in their gondolas. Although huge motorboats tend to spoil the view, you can still see gondolas against the light of the fireworks illuminating the lagoon, and people do go and decorate their boats with lights and greenery, and eat out on the water waiting for the fireworks.

Lady Layard and her friends went out in a gondola, on July 18, 1885:

> There were quantities of gondolas and a great many of them were decorated with garlands and chinese lanterns. In the big boats – there was generally a table round which people sat and supped. After the fireworks we met at a trysting place and it being to early for supper separating again and rowed about to see the boats and the crowd. The bridges of boats are at usual places across the Grand Canal and the Giudecca for the foot passengers. The scene was a very animated one and there was singing and gaiety in every direction. At 12.30 our gondolas met again and we tied them one to another and anchored and then prepared to sup by putting boards across the gondolas and so we had the appearance of being seated on each side of a long table.

The next day Lady Layard annotated that the young people had gone out to see the sun rise at the Lido, "as the Venetians do".

James wrote about the Redentore in the essay *The Grand Canal:*

> The feast of the Redeemer – the great popular feast of the year – is a wonderful venetian Vauxhall. All Venice on this occasion takes to the boats for the night and loads them with lamps and provisions. Wedged together in a mass it sups and sings; every boat is a floating arbour, a private *café-concert*. Of all Christian commemorations it is the most ingenuously and harmlessly pagan. Toward morning the passengers repair to the Lido, where, as the sun rises, they plunge, still sociably, into the sea. The night of the Redentore has been described, but it would be interesting to have an account from a domestic point of view, of its usual morrow. It is mainly an affair of the Giudecca, however, which is bridged over from the Zattere to the great church. The pontoons are laid together during the day – it is all done with extraordinary celerity and art – and the bridge is prolonged across the Canalazzo (to Santa Maria Zobenigo), which is my only warrant for glancing at the occasion. We glance at it from our palace windows; lengthening our necks a little, as we look up towards the Salute, we see all Venice, on the July afternoon, so serried as to move slowly, pour across the temporary footway. It is a flock of very good children, and the bridged Grand Canal is their toy. All Venice on such occasions is gentle and friendly; not even all Venice pushes one into the water (*The Grand Canal*, 41-42).

You will find that Venice is "gentle and friendly" on such an occasion, even if you don't have James's privileged viewpoint from the balcony of the Palazzo Barbaro.

*****

The danger is that you will not linger enough…(*Venice,* 4).

At my *moments perdus* I think lots and lots about Venice – which was really the most refined and romantic little time that I had during my *Italienische Reise.* Every hour of it comes back to me – every twist and turn of our charming little smelling explorations; every cool dip into every damp old chapel; every tiptoe evasion from the vigilance of the Angel (*Letters to Miss Allen,* 14, August 26, 1899).

The Angel was, of course, Mrs. Curtis, from whose protection James liked to escape at times, but whose Palazzo Barbaro was James's favourite residence and the palace that acted most powerfully on his imagination.

Works cited.

Henry James:
The Aspern Papers:
  The Turn of the Screw and *The Aspern papers,* London, Everyman's Library, 1963.
Autobiography:
  Autobiography, Frederick W. Dupee ed., Princeton, Princeton University Press, 1983.
Cara Donna Isabella:
  Cara Donna Isabella, Lettere a Isabella Stewart Gardner, Rosella Mamoli Zorzi ed., Milano, Archinto, 2004.
Casa Alvisi:
  Italian Hours, New York, Grove Press, 1909.
The Chaperon:
  Complete Stories 1884-1891, Edward Said ed., New York, The Library of America, 1999.
George Sand:
  Literary Criticism. French Writers, Other European Writers, The Prefaces to the New York Edition, Leon Edel ed., with the assistance of Mark Wilson, New York, The Library of America, 1984.
The Grand Canal:
  Italian Hours, New York, Grove Press, 1909.
LBP:
  Letters from the Palazzo Barbaro, Rosella Mamoli Zorzi ed., London, Pushkin Press, 1998.
Letters:
  Henry James, Letters, 4 vols., Leon Edel ed., Cambridge, The Belknap Press of Harvard University Press, 1974-1984.
Letters to Miss Allen:
  Lettere a Miss Allen 1899-1915, Letters to Miss Allen 1899-1915, Rosella Mamoli Zorzi ed., Milano, Archinto, 1993.
Notebooks:
  The Complete Notebooks of Henry James, Leon Edel and Lyall H.Powers eds., Oxford U.P., 1987.
Preface to *Portrait of a Lady:*
  Literary Criticism. French Writers, Other European Writers, The Prefaces to the New York Edition, Leon Edel ed., with the assistance of Mark Wilson, New York, The Library of America, 1984.
Preface to *the Spoils of Poynton, A London Life, The Chaperon:*
  Literary Criticism. French Writers, Other European Writers, The Prefaces to the New York Edition, Leon Edel ed., with the assistance of Mark Wilson, New York, The Library of America, 1984.
Princess Casamassima:
  Novels 1886-1890, Daniel Mark Fogel ed., New York, The Library of America, 1989.

The Pupil:
> *Complete Stories 1884-1891,* Edward Said ed., New York, The Library of America, 1999.

Travelling Companions:
> *Complete Stories 1864-1874,* Daniel Mark Fogel ed., New York, The Library of America, 1989.

Two Old Houses and Three Young Women:
> *Italian Hours,* New York, Grove Press, 1909.

Venice:
> *Italian Hours,* New York, Grove Press, 1909.

Venice, An early Impression:
> *Italian Hours,* New York, Grove Press, 1909.

William Wetmore Story and his Friends:
> *William Wetmore Story and his Friends,* London, Thames and Hudson, 1903.

The Wings of the Dove:
> *The Wings of the Dove,* J. Donald Crowley and Richard A. Hocks eds., New York, Norton, 2003.

Other primary works cited:

Enid Layard, *The Diary* (Browning Armstrong Library e-text).
John Ruskin, *The Stones of Venice,* 3 vols., London, George Allen and Unwin, 1925.

Selected bibliography.

Works by Henry James.
Letters:
Edel, Leon, ed., *Letters,* 4 vols., Cambridge, The Belknap Press of Harvard University Press, 1974-1984.
Edel, Leon ed., *Selected Letters,* The Belknap Press of Harvard U.P., 1987.
Gunter, Susan, ed., *Dear Munificent Friends: Henry James's Letters to Four Women.* Ann Arbor, University of Michigan Press, 1999.
Gunter, Susan E. and Steven H. Jobe, eds. *Dearly Beloved Friends. Henry James's Letters to Younger Men,* Ann Arbor, The University of Michigan Press, 2001.
Horne, Philip, ed., *Henry James. A Life in Letters,* London, Allen Lane, 1999.
Lubbock, Percy, ed., *The Letters of Henry James.* 2 vols., London, Scribner's, 1920.
Mamoli Zorzi, Rosella, ed., *Lettere a Miss Allen, Letters to Miss Allen,* Milano, Archinto, 1993.
— *Lettere da Palazzo Barbaro,* Milano, Archinto, 1989; English edition: *Letters from the Palazzo Barbaro,* London, Pushkin Press, 1998.
— *Amato ragazzo. Lettere a Hendrik C. Andersen 1899-1915,* Venezia, Marsilio, 2000; American edition: *Beloved Boy, Letters to Hendrik C. Andersen, 1899-1915, Introduction to the English Edition by* Millicent Bell, *with an Afterword by* Elena di Majo, Charlottesville, University of Virginia Press, 2004.

Other works by Henry James:
Leon Edel ed., *The American Scene*, Bloomington, Indiana University Press, 1968.
John L. Sweeney ed., *The Painter's Eye,* Foreword by Susan M. Griffin, The University of Wisconsin Press, 1989.

Selected Critical Works:
Auchard, John, *Introduction and Notes* to *Italian Hours,* John Auchard ed., University Park, Pennsylvania, Pennsylvania State University Press, 1992
Battilana, Marilla, *Venezia sfondo e simbolo nella narrativa di Henry James,* Milano, Laboratorio delle Arti, 1971.
Chong, Alan, and Richard Lingner, Elizabeth Anne McCauley, Rosella Mamoli Zorzi eds., *Gondola Days. Isabella Stewart Gardner and the Palazzo Barbaro Circle,* The Isabella Stewart Gardner Museum, Boston, Distributed by Antique Collectors' Club, 2004.
Hadley, Rollin van N. ed., *The Letters of Bernard Berenson and Isabella Stewart Gardner,* 1887-1924, with Correspondence by Mary Berenson, Boston, Northeastern U.P., 1987.
Kilmurray, Elaine and Richard Ormond eds., *Sargent,* Tate Gallery Publishing, 1998.
Mamoli Zorzi, Rosella, *Robert Browning a Venezia* (cat. di mostra), Venezia, Fondazione Scientifica Querini Stampalia, 1989.
— *The Pastimes of Culture. The Tableaux Vivants of the British Expatriates in Venice in the 1880s and 1890s,* in *Textus,* XII, 1, 1999, pp. 77-96.
— *Art in the museums and art in the homes. Tableaux Vivants in Isabella Stewart Gardner's time,* in *Annali di Ca' Foscari,* 41, 2002, pp. 63-89.
— "*Gondola Days*". *Isabella Stewart Gardner e il suo mondo a Palazzo Barbaro-Curtis,* Edizioni della Laguna, 2004.
Meredith, Michael, ed., *More than Friend. The Letters of Robert Browning to Katharine de Kay Bronson,* Armstrong Browning Library and Wedgestone Press, 1985.
Montanaro, Carlo, *Il cinema a Venezia,* in *Modigliani a Venezia, tra Livorno e Parigi,* Christian Parisot ed., Sassari, Delfino Editore, 2005, pp. 181-183.
Pemble, John, *Venice Rediscovered,* Oxford, The Clarendon Press, 1995.
Perosa, Sergio, ed., *Henry James e Venezia,* Firenze, Leo Olschki, 1987.
Tanner, Tony, *Venice Desired,* Cambridge, Harvard University Press, 1992.
Tintner, Adeline, *The Museum World of Henry James,* UMI Research Press, 1986.
Tuttleton James and Agostino Lombardo eds., *The Sweetest Impression of Life. The James Family and Italy,* New York, New York University Press, 1990.

Biographies:
Edel, Leon, *Henry James,* 5 vols., Philadelphia, Lippincott, 1953-1972.
Edel, Leon, *Henry James, A Life,* New York, Harper and Row, 1985.
Gordon, Lyndall, *A Private Life of Henry James, Two Women and His Art,* London, Chatto and Windus, 1998.
Kaplan, Fred, *Henry James, The Imagination of Genius,* New York, William Morrow, 1992.
Novick, Sheldon M., *Henry James, The Young Master,* New York, Random House, 1996.

Books on Venice:

Bassi, Elena, *Palazzi di Venezia,* Venezia, La Stamperia di Venezia Editrice, 1976.
Bernardello, Adolfo, "Venezia 1830-1866. Iniziative economiche, accumulazione e investimenti di capitale", in *Il Risorgimento,* 1-2, 2002, pp. 5-56.
Goffen, Rona, *Giovanni Bellini,* Milano, Federico Motta Editore, 1990.
Honour, Hugh and John Fleming, *The Venetian Hours of Henry James,* London, Walker Books, 1991.
Isnenghi Mario and Stuart Woolf, eds., *Storia di Venezia. L'Ottocento e il Novecento,* 2 vols., Roma, Istituto della Enciclopedia Italiana, 2002.
Lorenzetti, Giulio, *Venezia e il suo estuario,* Trieste, Lint, 1994.
Mangiarotti, Vittorio, *Guida commerciale di Venezia per l'anno 1869,* Venezia, Tipografia Cecchini, 1869.
Murray, John, *Handbook for Travellers in Northern Italy,* London, John Murray, 1869.
Norwich, John Julius, *Paradise of Cities,* London, Viking, 2003.
Nuova guida di Venezia, n.p., 1861.
Pallucchini, Rodolfo and Paola Rossi, *Tintoretto. Le opere sacre e profane,* 2 vols., Milano, Alfieri-Electa, 1982.
Petri, Rolf, "La sfida lagunare: investimenti e imprenditori stranieri a Venezia", in *Padania,* 4, 1988, pp. 57-96.
Querini Stampalia, Andrea, *Nuova guida annuale di Venezia,* Venezia, premiata Tipografia di Giovanni Cecchini, 1856.
Romanelli, Giandomenico, *Venezia Ottocento,* Roma, Officina editore, 1977.
—   *Venezia nell'Ottocento: immagini e mito,* Milano, Electa, 1983.
—   *Le Due dame veneziane,* Milano, Silvanaeditoriale-Sole 24-ore, 2003.
—   ed., *Palazzo Ducale: storia e restauri,* Verona, Arsenale, 2004.
Scirè Nepi, Giovanna, *Gallerie dell'Accademia di Venezia,* Milano, Electa, 1998.
Sgarbi, Vittorio, *Carpaccio,* Milano, Fabbri, 1994.
Tassini, Giuseppe, *Curiosità Veneziane,* Elio Zorzi ed., Venezia, Scarabellin, 1933.
Una città e il suo museo. Un secolo e mezzo di collezioni civiche veneziane, Venezia, Museo Correr, 1988.
Venezia. Il Canal Grande, Il Gazzettino illustrato, n.d., n.p.
Zangirolami, Cesare, *Indicatore anagrafico e guida pratica di Venezia,* Venezia, Soc. An. Industrie Grafiche, 1921.
Zorzi, Alvise, *Canal Grande,* Milano, Rizzoli, 1991.
—   *Venezia austriaca 1798-1866,* Roma-Bari, Laterza, 1985.